The Frontier and
Canadian Letters

THE FRONTIER
AND
CANADIAN LETTERS

Wilfrid Eggleston

With an Introduction by D. O. Spettigue

The Carleton Library No. 102

Published by McClelland and Stewart Limited
in association with the Institute of
Canadian Studies, Carleton University

THE CARLETON LIBRARY
A series of original works, reprints and new
collections of source material relating to
Canada, issued under the editorial supervision
of the Institute of Canadian Studies of
Carleton University, Ottawa.

DIRECTOR OF THE INSTITUTE
Davidson Dunton

GENERAL EDITOR
Michael G. Gnarowski

EXECUTIVE EDITOR
James H. Marsh

EDITORIAL BOARD
B. Carman Bickerton (*History*)
Dennis Forcese (*Sociology*)
David B. Knight (*Geography*)
J. George Neuspiel (*Law*)
Thomas K. Rymes (*Economics*)
Derek G. Smith (*Anthropology*)
Michael S. Whittington (*Political Science*)

The Frontier and Canadian Letters was first
published in 1957 by The Ryerson Press,
Toronto. It is republished in this edition by
permission of the author and first publisher.

ISBN 0-7710-9805-7

The Canadian Publishers
McClelland and Stewart Limited
25 Hollinger Road, Toronto

Printed and bound in Canada

CONTENTS

The following acknowledgement appeared in the
original edition.

In a work of scholarship the author is universally permitted to
quote brief extracts of both prose and verse. Every care has been
taken in this monograph to acknowledge title, author and publisher at the exact place of quotation. Both author and publisher
gladly acknowledge their thanks to the many authors and publishers indicated in this book. They request information which will
enable them to correct any credit in the next edition.

Introduction to the Carleton Library Edition

It is a privilege to introduce this important study by Wilfrid Eggleston to the generation of readers that follows his. When *The Frontier and Canadian Letters* was published in 1957, the long drought in Canadian Studies was about to end. Malcolm Ross was just launching the New Canadian Library, first of the series of paperback reprints, soon to include the Carleton Library, which for over two decades now have made Canadian texts available as they never had been before, and so made possible the unprecedented expansion of Canadian studies in the universities in the 'sixties and in the schools in the 'seventies. Until 1957, the paperback revolution had not yet democratized Canadian studies, nor had the series of critical letters and the new critical magazines appeared. The university quarterlies (Queen's, Toronto, Dalhousie) had allowed some Canadian content for decades, and then as now there were the little magazines to sustain the hopes of the young and the daring. *Canadian Forum* carried on undaunted, but the courageous editors of such periodicals as *First Statement*, *Northern Review* and *Contemporary Verse* had had their day, and in the early 1950's the future did not look bright for critical magazines. The run of new critical periodicals was signalled when *Tamarack Review* came boldly, not to say brashly, on to the scene in 1957. George Woodcock's *Canadian Literature* appeared in 1959; the first of the university periodicals devoted exclusively to Canadian Studies, its advent marked the modern phase of academic respectability in Canadian Studies. One suspects that university expansion and general affluence, often in the form of Canada Council or Arts Council support, had much to do with the subsequent development, which has seen in the past five years such periodicals as the *Journal of Canadian Fiction* and *Studies in Canadian Literature* launched while countless little magazines came out of the garrets to parade glossily on the bookshelves. Harder times may send many of them back into their garrets, if not into limbo, again.

The Frontier and Canadian Letters marked the divide between the contemporary era of paperback and periodical proliferation and the previous one of rare but often impressive publications by the committed few who, like the critics of old, took Canadian literature as their province almost as a recreation from their public duties. Such were Alfred Bailey, E. K. Brown, W. E. Collin, Northrop Frye, R. Gustafson, C. F. Klinck, Desmond Pacey, Gordon Roper, A. J. M. Smith, F. R. Scott, R. E. Watters, A. S. P. Woodhouse and all those who were the editors of anthologies, of literary journals and of annual reviews of Canadian letters in the 'forties and 'fifties, and the authors of critical biographies and studies of writers whose names they kept alive. Poets themselves sometimes, and leading academics trained to the study of English literature, they brought mature judgment to the criticism of individual writers before the broad thematic studies such as this one could be made.

The context for Wilfrid Eggleston's book is sufficiently indicated in his own Introduction. It assumes the validity of science and its application to social studies. It assumes a common colonial experience in the younger nations that began as European outposts. It assumes the worth of the arts but insists that these are social phenomena. In essence it asks, What were the conditions in the mother countries under which literature flourished? And then it examines a given colony at a given moment to see if those conditions yet obtain. It is an appropriate book for a professional journalist to have written, and a journalist moreover, steeped in the lore of his own country and embodying in himself, as he observes, its almost instantaneous transition from pioneer to urban conditions.

Inevitably its antecedents are American. Because the great republic has preceded us along most roads, we have tended to follow American signposts, whether we are holding a political convention or adapting TV entertainment or writing literary history.

Mr. Eggleston acknowledges many of the critical and historical sources from which he benefited, from L. A. White's *The Science of Culture* to E. K. Brown's *On Canadian Poetry*. Of course the grandfathers of all such North American studies are V. L. Parrington's *Main Currents in American Thought*, Vol. I, James Truslow Adams' *The Epic of America* and *Provincial Society 1690-1763*, and above all Frederick Jackson Turner's *The Frontier in American History*. From these giants we learned that North American democracy was fostered by free land on a moving frontier; that as the frontier moved westward the more venturesome immigrants gravitated to it while the more conservative element built up the older settled areas; that subsequent political and social developments were predicated on this economic thesis; that "culture"—meaning primarily the evidences of esthetic taste founded on the traditions of the arts in Europe—was built up in older areas progressively in imitation of Old-World models, after a sufficient period of growth, stability, accumulated wealth, leisure, educational and religious institutions, communications and other services made cultivation of the intellect and the emotions an acceptable luxury. On the frontier, of course, they were inadmissable luxuries, and the frontier habit of practicality would always make the arts suspect in colonial popular culture.

From these sources, too, we learned to apply the botanical analogy that sees emigration as a transplanting into a new soil. At first, according to this metaphor, the transplanted stock withers under the shock of being uprooted and thrust into alien soil. If it survives, it may remain dormant for years before it renews its growth. By analogy, a transplanted culture also withers, shedding some of its ways as it leaves behind some of its goods, and finding others inappropriate to its new environment. So the society transplanted to the eastern American seaboard, initially vigorous, declined culturally to a nadir in the early 18th century before reasserting itself and, by the 19th century, acquiring a recognizable culture and producing a literature of its own, the "Flowering of New England", as Van Wyck Brooks calls it.

Of course there were many subsequent refinements of these formative studies, applying the economic premise, the botanical analogy and the adaptation hypothesis. Harold Innis's *Fur Trade in Canada*, along with Donald Creighton, had argued for the

"Laurentian" as opposed to the "continental" axis; Louis B. Wright's *Culture on the Moving Frontier* stressed the continuity of European culture in the homes and institutions of the New World, as did J. P. Matthews' *Tradition in Exile* for the Australian and Canadian scenes. R. E. Rashley's *Poetry in Canada: The First Three Steps* followed Parrington and Wright, and so in effect does *The Frontier and Canadian Letters*. Borrowing the botanical analogy, Mr. Eggleston asks:

> what spiritual soil and what climate had produced great eras of literature elsewhere and in older times? And what social *milieu*, what cultural atmosphere, would have to be evolved by the migrants of the old societies to North America, before a sophisticated and refined product like *belles lettres* could be expected?

What follows must be a "study of environment," but Mr. Eggleston points out that, despite recent advances, social studies of the diverse regions of Canada were not yet adequate in 1957 for such an analysis as he felt should be made. His work, therefore, could only point the way, while examining closely the literary milieux of the few writers whose educational, social, domestic and artistic contexts were already documented.

Necessarily, the availability of documentation in part determined, or limited, the scope of the book. The Fredericton circle had been looked at, by Bailey, Cappon, and others, the early Halifax flowering by Chittick, the Lakefield group by Needler, and individual studies had been made of Richardson, of Kirby, of Lampman, of Grove, of Pratt. Because no information was available on literary developments in Newfoundland or the Pacific Coast, and little on the prairies, the "full-fledged examination of the origins of Canada's literature" that Mr. Eggleston anticipated could not yet be written. Within a decade of the publication of *The Frontier and Canadian Letters*, Carl Klinck's *Literary History of Canada* would help to fill some of the gaps, but at the same time the outburst of new writing in the 'sixties and 'seventies would change the scene Mr. Eggleston had so carefully studied.

The Frontier and Canadian Letters is therefore a study, at a particular stage of Canadian criticism, of Canadian literature at a particular stage: an attempt to account for a largely colonial literature made as the colonial era belatedly ended. True to Canadian traditions, that era did not end with any eclat; the writing simply increased in quantity and quality at a rate and in an atmosphere that have made earlier generalizations less relevant.

Mr. Eggleston takes a long perspective of his subject, drawing from the authorities on early American literature for the observation that, though the beginnings of settlement were made in the days of Shakespeare, Spenser, Milton, for 200 years the young nation produced no belles lettres of any significance. He notes that the explanations traditionally offered for that failure—a hard life, a harsh climate, the primacy of material needs, the lack of the means of distribution, competition from the mother country—are the same ones offered by apologists for Canadian literature into the 20th century. If the American colonies could not produce literary masterpieces, how could the Canadian, where conditions were even less auspicious? But Mr. Eggleston is not satisfied with the American excuses any more than the Canadian, and he turns back to the botanical analogy for something more illuminating.

His second chapter, therefore, "Climate and Soil in Literary Flowerings," goes to Turner and even to the anthropologists for observations on neolithic culture in early North America, primitive conditions that determined that "at the frontier, the environment is at first too strong for the man;" he must accept the condition which it furnishes, or perish. This means abandoning Old World tools, dress, manners, refinements of language, social assumptions, whatever interferes with the overriding need to survive. And as long as mere survival values obtained, there might be individual artists struggling in isolation but there would be little overt evidence of the arts of civilization.

> Before a golden Age, or, for that matter, any kind of Age of Polite Letters could be looked for on North American soil, it would be necessary for the colonists and settlers to import or bring into being in a new continent at least some of the cultural and technical equipment and environment which had assisted in all the literary movements of Europe, but which, over there, had required several thousand years of growth and evolution.

Like his predecessors, Mr. Eggleston asks why a long hiatus—the familiar "cultural lag"—was necessary before a sufficient North American "culture" existed to make a literary flowering possible or to produce a new flame. He does not examine the possibility that the New World might never repeat the circumstances of the Old; that the age of the printed word might, as Marshall McLuhan suggested, be over; that there might therefore never be in North America or in other European offshoots, a civilization comparable to the parent civilization; and that there might never be another literary renascence anywhere.

Canadian studies, as Michael Cross has shown, express many of the same assumptions, in the same terms, as Turner; perhaps these were post-Rousseau clichés in the European, and hence the emigrant, mind. But to settlers in Canada, recently arrived from Europe, the New World often seemed less than dynamically ideal. Conditions on the frontier—if by that we mean areas in the first phase of clearing or breaking land and building lean-to's and shacks—often seemed to encourage the vices more evidently than the virtues. Early writers like Anna Jameson and Susanna Moodie noted the tendency to drunkenness, violence and sloth. Mrs. Moodie's "Yankee"—i.e. late Loyalist—neighbours represent for her the sacrifice of manners, morals, language, taste, the decencies, under the levelling (and deadening) influence of the frontier. Turner and his successors also acknowledged the "return to barbarism" that sometimes resulted from frontier conditions and that in some areas survives today. The message of Mrs. Moodie's *Roughing It in the Bush* is that, if barbarism is the price of adaptation to the new environment, then the cost is too high. The difference is that between the progressive and the conservative positions. Traditionally—though the tradition should not go unchallenged—American literature has preferred the forward-looking, Canadian literature the retrospective, position.

In his introductory enquiry into the general characteristics of colonial societies, Mr. Eggleston observes that the "smallest unity of society is the family. . . . The spiritual drive and subsequent career of the incipient writer may have been essentially fixed and settled before the child moves out into the larger community surrounding his home." Hence "some consideration of the pioneer family" must be included, and beyond it the shaping community. He quotes White:

If the individual is born and reared in a frontier culture where life is hard and hazardous, where a keen eye and a quick trigger are prized, where hard drinking and harder fighting are manly virtues, and where a square dance to a squeaky fiddle is the highest form of art, he is not likely to achieve fame as a poet, composer, sculptor, philosopher or scientist.

Noting the rise in literary activity in New England after the Revolution, Eggleston catalogues the necessary conditions:

an accumulation of wealth and the possibility of leisure and travel, a revival of zeal for education and erudition, the launching of literary magazines, the appearance of one or two outstanding teachers, the creation of clubs and cultural societies, and the enlargement of the literary market to the point where professional men and women of letters might subsist and even flourish. As important as the financial rewards were the prizes of prestige and esteem.

The question then must be, when were such conditions realized in Canada? Mr. Eggleston confronts immediately the "flowering" of Halifax with Howe and Haliburton "less than two generations" after the coming of the Loyalists, that is, relatively much earlier than the first flowerings of New England. The explanations offered are not convincing nor does the apparent phenomenon itself recognize the counter-argument offered, that Port Royal was founded in 1605, so Nova Scotia was even older than New England as a white settlement. More probably, the sea-links with New York and Boston, and less directly with Britain, were the stimulus for what there was of Maritime culture.

Upper Canada is treated as the closest equivalent to the American frontier. The hardships of pioneer life—including the prohibitive cost of postage and candles (both necessities for literary aspirants)—are offered as explanations for the relative poverty of literary output even by immigrant authors. The wonder is that so much was written. But because the inland regions were so much more isolated and remote from cultural contact, any "flowering" had longer to wait than in the Maritimes, and in Ontario the hostility to the arts was more obvious. How, then, to account for

Maj. John Richardson? The simplest answer, I suppose, is that the officer-class of the garrisons was a cultural stimulus of sorts, as it was at the same time in Halifax. Mr. Eggleston prefers to fall back on the presence of Richardson's alleged aristocratic French mother. The danger of this type of explanation becomes apparent in Pacey's revelation that Richardson's grandmother in fact was Amerindian. She might well be the explanation, insofar as a single fact can be, but not of a kind to support Mr. Eggleston's argument for cultural continuity with Europe.

Chapter VII attempts "to illustrate the frontier thesis" by a few notes on the early letters of French-speaking Canada. The same stultifying influences of the frontier are called upon to account for the absence of an early French-Canadian literary tradition, but more so: "Is a native literature remotely possible without even a single printer, a single publisher or a single bookstore in the community?" And when the conquest brought the means of literary publication in its wake, the temper of the people inevitably was directed toward the past. Here, more recent scholarship and the flood of new writers might give a very different picture; but of course this book is concerned with the pioneer phase, or phases, only.

The Fredericton writers of the 1880's are treated as a family group within a small but college-centered community whose cohesion could "ignite, but could not feed, the literary flame." Emphasis is put on the strong, conservative educational background that led to Roberts' role as a founding father of Canadian literature. This was not in any sense a pioneer community, and yet the capital, Fredericton, had a population of only 6000 at that time. None of the Fredericton group, Mr. Eggleston observes, was able to earn a living by writing.

"Ontario society was singularly slow to produce a climate and soil favourable to the growth of native arts and letters," Mr. Eggleston writes in his chapter, "Frontier Values Outlive the Frontier." Here the botanical analogy seems most apt, for after the initial production by literary immigrants like Moodie (and after precocious blooms like Richardson) there is a noticeable withering to the end of the nineteenth century, and renewed growth is slow in the twentieth. For the few names that do appear, the explanation offered is "family influences, supplemented by cultural stimuli brought in from the outside world." For Canadian nationalists Mr. Eggleston's message is clear: the arts will not thrive in isolation.

"The Last Great Frontier" Mr. Eggleston examines is the Canadian West, where the same phases had to be gone through but where, except for a few early pockets of settlement, the transition from wilderness to modern urbanised life took place within a single lifetime. Admittedly the number of cities was small. Much of the West, Eggleston points out, is as sparsely settled as Siberia and just as unlikely to foster any literature.

> You could spend half a lifetime in that rangeland setting without ever seeing a play, hearing a lyric well read, meeting an author, browsing in a bookstore, seeing a publisher, attending a literary society, or talking with a literary critic.... What a contrast, and how remote from the Boston of, say, 1830!

Mr. Eggleston glances at Connor, Begg, McClung, Salverson, Stead, Grove and others as precursors of a literature that never really flowered. (Today, such names as those of Margaret Laurence, Rudy Wiebe, Robert Kroetsch, George Ryga, and Sheila Watson challenge critics like William New and John Moss to explain the vigour of western writing. But with only McCourt's *The Canadian West in Fiction* as his guide, Mr. Eggleston could not have anticipated such a development.) He gives Grove slightly more attention than the others, and here the biographical facts (pp. 145-148) need some correction. Grove was 34 (not 21 or 40) when he came to Manitoba to live. The account of his "struggling on alone for nearly thirty years" in the West before learning how to prepare a manuscript is fiction; Grove had been a professional man of letters before he came to Canada, and he came here twenty years later than his autobiography claimed. Whether or not they were "useful" to him, his prose models were the English classics. The "chance encounter" that "put him right" about manuscripts probably is apocryphal, and the late Arthur Phelps assured me that Lorne Pierce's presence at that Winnipeg meeting of 1924 was "not quite by chance." Moreover, Phelps and Kirkconnell worked hard to attract the "chance" interest of the Canadian Clubs.

There are other observations that time has invalidated. Sinclair Ross, for example, ceased to be a "one-book author", even though most readers still prefer his first book. These do not, however, invalidate Mr. Eggleston's study. We could add many and prouder new names to his "proud names," and possibly would delete a few that have not worn well. We could add the names of newer and, in some cases, better magazines than were open to the writer in 1957. And, as Mr. Eggleston exclaims, "there is the Canada Council!" That there has to be a Canada Council, of course, may only bear out the thesis that our meagre soil is not of itself likely to hold much promise for the arts. "We publish, in all languages," he reports, "about 600 titles a year, of which four million copies are printed. This sounds well. However, it is about one-sixth of the comparable total for Belgium and about one-ninth the production in the Netherlands." We might add the recent statistic that of some $180,000,000 worth of books sold annually in Canada now, $120,000,000 are handled by American owned publishing companies. Our economic colonialism may not have ended yet, and may never end.

Mr. Eggleston concludes by raising again the question he poses throughout his study: how to account for the relative poverty of the arts, in Canada and North America. Perhaps, he suggests, this continent is inherently hostile to the arts and never will support such literatures as were the glories of Europe. Perhaps the legacy of the frontier will be the dethronement of literature from the high place it once held in Western culture. Certainly the spread of American culture around the world will mean that those values the American frontier allegedly nurtured will, for better or worse, be everyone's values tomorrow. Perhaps they have hastened the demise of the printed word.

It seems unlikely. Since 1957, the decline of poetry lamented by Mr. Eggleston has, according to outward signs, stopped and even reversed its trend. Poetry as a spoken art has been successfully revived. More magazines and more books are published, more support is available to authors and editors. Insofar as a conscious government policy can prevail against indifference, progress is being made. But still the indifference—the doubt about the validity of the arts—is there. Recently a school near my home advertized an evening public-interest course in Canadian Literature. The course had been well prepared, and was sufficiently announced. Yet it had to be cancelled: not a single registration was received. Perhaps all the arts exist only because a small intellectual community—the "vertical society" this book ends with—considers them important. Where that community becomes too small, as in the impersonal electronic age it may do, then the conditions of the frontier might obtain again, whatever the supposed compensations, and the cultural life of the whole community could again decline.

I say "could" because this could happen; but I am confident it will not. Art is no stranger to adversity. If it can survive in a physically hostile environment it can survive in our artificial environment where the enemies are lip-service and popular misconceptions, misdirected support and political expediency, superficial education and control by a bureaucracy in league with the commercial media. There is a sense in which the arts are always on a frontier, always opposed by a narrow utility and expediency. There is also a sense in which the arts are continually pressing back the frontiers of experience, and this is the direction in which today's commentator would enlarge Mr. Eggleston's thesis. Not only would he add the new poets and playwrights—there were few of the latter visible in 1957—the writers of Newfoundland, the young Quebec activists, and the whole creative movement of the West Coast in the 60's, he would show how Davies and Watson, Wiebe, Kroetsche, Laurence, Ryga, Reaney, Avison, Atwood, Blais, Aquin, Carrier, Hood, Bowering, Newlove, Helwig, Metcalf, and so many others are exploring the omnipresent frontiers of consciousness and finding the forms to express them. When the physical frontiers have receded—Mowat, Purdy, Theriault and others have pursued them into the Arctic—the emotional frontiers remain as part of the contemporary, and the national, consciousness. These are always here to explore, in terms appropriate to each new generation, and the artists will be, as they always have been, the adventurous frontiersmen prepared to settle them and move with them as they recede. With this qualification, *The Frontier and Canadian Letters* remains as pertinent to today's, as to Wilfrid Eggleston's, generation of Canadians.

The text printed here is that of the 1957 edition, without altera-
tion.

D. O. SPETTIGUE

Queen's University
February, 1976

INTRODUCTION

SEVERAL YEARS ago I gave a series of talks on early Canadian writing, in the extension programme of Carleton College (now Carleton University). In preparation for these, I went back to all the accounts I could lay my hands on, some of which I had read in my undergraduate days. I found the circumstances of pioneer writing a fascinating subject, perhaps partly so because my own boyhood had been spent on the frontier range in south-eastern Alberta. Several things struck me with particular force. There was the long delay in the emergence of a true native literature in British North America. However, when I looked at the story of native letters in other colonial areas I found that there was nothing unusual about this retardation; indeed, it was typical. Another interesting point was the way in which a note of defensiveness, of apology, and extenuation, kept appearing in the native accounts of Canadian letters. Every one seemed to expect that Canada should soon develop a notable literature. Why? Because the immigrant stock came from nations long famous for their poetry, drama, fiction and essays. Canada was still too young and too thinly populated, it was said, but with age and numbers she too would produce Shakespeares and Balzacs.

After I had read half a dozen surveys of Canadian literature, I began to wonder whether a fresh approach might not throw new light on the story. E. K. Brown and A. G. Bailey, in particular, had suggested a treatment of the history of literature as one of the flowerings of a complex society, rather than as a compilation of biographical details of isolated individuals. If the literary historian were to come to his consideration of *belles lettres* fresh from a study of the larger social history of North America, it should be more fruitful, I thought. Literature as a social and cultural flower in turn suggested the botanical analogy: what spiritual soil and what climate had produced great eras of literature elsewhere and in older times? And what social *milieu*, what cultural atmosphere, would have to be evolved by the migrants of the old societies to North America, before a sophisticated and refined product like *belles lettres* could be expected? Was such a soil and climate to be found anywhere in British North America in the nineteenth century? At any rate there were interesting associations of native writers, first at Halifax in the 1820's and 1830's, then at Quebec City two or three decades later, and at Fredericton in the 1880's. Upper Canada had its isolated literary "accidents" such as Richardson and Sangster, but little evidence of literary societies.

Such speculations led me to attempt a brief re-examination of the main events of Canadian letters in the frontier days and in the generations immediately following. *The Frontier and Canadian Letters* is really a reconnaisance rather than a scholarly assault on the theme, but I hope that it may encourage more methodical and painstaking investigations of our literary heritage and tradition. The study of environment has made notable strides since most of our chronicles of Canadian letters were written. I was considerably fortified in theories which I had worked out earlier, when in 1956, with a first draft complete, I came upon Leslie A. White's work, *The Science of Culture* (New York, 1949), to which I am much indebted for some lines in Chapter III. Behind any literary burgeoning in a relatively new land there must be a long period of preparation and insemination. There are essential prerequisites, such as schools, libraries, printing presses, book-shops, a receptive society, publishers and critics. A full-fledged examination of the origins of Canada's literature would include the story of printing and publishing in Canada, an account of her more stimulating teachers, an investigation of the influence of books and libraries, and the contributions of critics. Even more illuminating might be a study of the larger society and its dominating values.

The Frontier and Canadian Letters is illustrative, of course, and not definitive. I have presented such illustrations as I could find. If some areas are treated more fully than others, it is because the ground work has been done there by such historians as Dean

Bailey. I was unable to find the kind of study of Newfoundland's early literature which would have enabled me to include a section on it: I expect, however, the same general principles would be found to apply. I wish I could have added at least a few paragraphs on the literary society of the Pacific Coast. I hope that the illustrations that have been employed will be found to be suggestive and interesting.

I am grateful to all those who have authorized me to quote from their published works. I am conscious of an indebtedness to other writers and scholars, of this and earlier periods. I would single out in this connection the names of A. G. Bailey, James Truslow Adams, Leslie A. White, Van Wyck Brooks, E. K. Brown, Amram Scheinfeld, Carl F. Klinck, Carl Y. Connor, Mason Wade, E. A. McCourt, Vernon Parrington, F. J. Turner, Alexis Carrel, T. J. Wertenbaker, Carl Van Doren, Ray Palmer Baker, D. C. Harvey, W. E. Myatt, V. L. O. Chittick, J. W. Longley, Archibald MacMechan, E. M. Pomeroy, Sir John Willison, Marie Tremaine and Helen McCorquodale. To the warm encouragement and extensive research of Dr. Lorne Pierce I am particularly indebted. I should like also to thank the library staffs at Carleton University, Queen's, Mount Allison and the University of New Brunswick. My colleague, Dr. R. O. MacFarlane, brought to my attention some highly pertinent material about New England. In the preparation of the text the assistance of Lena and Anne was most acceptable.

WILFRID EGGLESTON

Carleton University
May, 1957,

CHAPTER I

A PLANT OF SLOW GROWTH

A PERSISTENT sense of inadequacy and apology runs through the early accounts of Canadian letters, interrupted occasionally by an outburst of shrill adolescent bragging. Perhaps in the nature of things this was inevitable, and arose from the background of the historians. Possibly all colonial art since the beginning of time has been viewed in this way. The first serious students of Canadian writing were almost inescapably *émigrés*, nurtured in a venerable tradition and disposed to look at all colonial efforts with a condescending eye. When native chroniclers appeared, they were apt to come to their examination of Canadian letters only after steeping themselves at school in the classics of Europe. Their norms and yardsticks were thus likely to be affected by their knowledge of Chaucer and Shakespeare, Molière and Balzac, Goethe and Heine.

Under these circumstances, some sense of uncertainty and inferiority, overcome at times by an upsurge of youthful arrogance, was probably to be expected. Whatever the explanation, such are the characteristic moods.

The underlying uneasiness comes out in various ways. One chronicler will ask anxiously why Canadian writing isn't better. Another will scold his compatriots for their low standards. There is a series of changes rung on the theme: Is there a Canadian Literature at all? Why is it so long in arriving? Now and again one finds a more charitable re-appraisal. Have our critics been too severe? Is our literature really better than we have supposed? Is it not possible that if we looked over our libraries and archives more carefully we would find neglected authors of great talent? And so on.

Unfortunately a cold-blooded re-appraisal of Canadian writing up to 1900 does very little to dispel the vague general impression that a literature of distinction and quality was very slow in making its appearance on British North American soil. If the search is for a strictly *native* literature, as distinct from the work of tourists, visitors, and *émigrés*—persons who brought their literary talents to this country fully developed—the body of meritorious work is small. If the search be further confined to work by native writers which is also the indubitable product of the Canadian environment, one is left with a few collections of poetry, three or four historical works, a few humorous sketches of enduring merit, and an essay or two, but not a single novel or play. It does not add up to a very impressive body of work.

In searching for this tiny collection, moreover, the historian will have found, particularly in the work published before 1880, a great quantity of second and third rate writing, crude, derivative, imitative, dull and stodgy. Much of it was old fashioned even when it was written. Native authors, before 1880, with two or three exceptions perhaps, lacked technical virtuosity. There are endless echoes of Goldsmith, Pope, Collins, Gray, Campbell, Moore, Byron and Burns.

In prose there are novels obviously, but insufficiently, inspired by Scott, Dumas and Fenimore Cooper.

This is a harsh indictment and may be resented. But even the most charitable survey cannot hide the fact that there was a long barren period in early writing, relieved here and there by a regional flowering of much merit. The existence of the long barren stretches seems to have thrown early historians on the defensive.

One defence was to make as much as possible of such figures as Alexander McLachlan, Charles Heavysege, William Kirby and Goldwin Smith, who, however, on closer examination could not be ranked as contributors to *native* letters at all. Another device was to offer plausible extenuations for past performances, closely coupled with an expression of faith in a Golden Age lying just ahead.

Many of these explanations seem now to have been wide of the mark. A more adequate grasp of the principles of social activity would have made them unnecessary. The cultural soil and climate of British North America was such as to make other productions than *belles lettres* likely.

Did not such historians proceed from faulty assumptions? Were they not still steeped in the Carlylean philosophy of individualism and the supremacy of the Great Man in history? Wherever a Great Man appeared, they felt, he made Great Events. It was Canada's tough luck that no Shakespeare or Scott had been born in "muddy" York or Bytown. When such Great Men emerged, we should have a worthy literature, no matter what the other circumstances might be.

The simple line of their reasoning can be readily traced. Canada, being a union of settlers from two great nations, both noted for their literature, would inevitably begin producing similar fine works on this side of the Atlantic as soon as the immigrants had been given a reasonable time to master the wilderness.

Time passed, but the miracle did not happen. Explanations lay conveniently to hand. The country was still too young. The population was still too small.

As the nineteenth century proceeded, such explanations sounded less convincing. The country was older now. The population mounted. Where were the literary giants?

By the middle of the nineteenth century, British North America's population far surpassed that of Attica at the time of Sophocles. By the end of the century Canada held more people than Elizabethan England. In 1903, the French-Canadians were celebrating three centuries on North American soil. By 1949, Halifax was celebrating its Bicentenary. How good were the stock apologies about age and population in the light of such facts?

The mood of the chroniclers can be illustrated by a few quotations.

In 1832, the editor of *The Canadian Casket* of Hamilton complained that his part of the country had not found a voice. He scolded his fellows, "descended from ancestors, who brought from the old world a portion of its literary treasures, Canadians have resembled more than a century past, persons who have been removed in childhood from the city to a desert . . . forgetful of the illustrious home and parentage from which they sprung."[1]

Three decades later, Edward Hartley Dewart, in the introduction to an anthology of Canadian poetry, wrote sadly: "There is probably no country in the world, making equal pretensions to intelligence and progress, where the claims of native literature are so little felt, and where every effort in poetry has been met with so much coldness and indifference, as in Canada."[2]

---

[1]Quoted by Carl F. Klinck: *Wilfred Campbell: A Study in Late Provincial Victorianism.* New York and Toronto, 1942. Pp. 2-3.
[2]*Selections from Canadian Poets*, Montreal, 1864.

Confederation was consummated in 1867, stirring up much nationalist sentiment. For a time it was believed that patriotism would inspire a new literature. The hope waned, and in 1881 John G. Bourinot (later Sir John) wrote that "it must be admitted that Canada has not yet produced any works which show a marked originality of thought." J. E. Collins, writing in *The Week* in 1884, observed that "the fiction and *belles lettres*, generally, have the limits of the municipality and the flavour of the log-hut."[1]

In 1887, George Stewart, Jr., addressing the Canadian Club in New York, said that "Canadian authorship is still in its infancy. . . . No one has been able . . . to make the writing of books his sole means of living . . . the business of publishing books in Canada is at a pretty low ebb . . . it is a fact that Canada cannot support a really first-class magazine. The experiment has been tried in all the chief centres of the Dominion, but it has failed in every instance, though the trial has been made honestly and at considerable sacrifice on the part of the promoters of the enterprise. . . . The market in Canada is limited, and, as a general rule, if a Canadian book is printed in Canada, little can be realized out of the venture." Like other honest but patriotic reporters, Stewart was impelled to add that there were encouraging developments and felt he was safe "in predicting that the day of successful Canadian authorship is not far distant."[2]

In the 1890's the inquest went on. We are told that Professor L. E. Horning of the University of Toronto circulated early in 1894 a questionnaire asking anxiously: "What is wrong with Canadian Literature?" Goldwin Smith is alleged to have retorted: "*What* Canadian Literature?" In another

[1]See "Literary Taste in Central Canada," by Claude T. Bissell, *Canadian Historical Review*, Vol. XXXI. P. 246.
[2]*Literature in Canada*, an address read before the Canadian Club of New York, 1887.

place his exact answer is reported to have included the
sentence: "No such thing as a literature in the local sense
exists or is ever likely to exist."[1]

Just before the end of the century (1898), Charles G. D.
Roberts (later Sir Charles) wrote in his *History of Canada:*

Literature has been a plant of slow growth on Canadian
soil. . . . In spite of obstacles, however, Canada has done
enough to show the strong imaginative and intellectual bent of
her people. . . . It must be remembered that the need of
literary expression could not arise very early in a people whose
energies were absorbed in the struggle for life, and whose
cravings for intellectual food had the literatures of France and
England to satisfy them.[2]

Spirits in Canada in the 1890's seem to have reached low
ebb and once into the twentieth century there was a change
of tone.   Canadian literature was reconsidered, and the idea
began to get some currency that it had been neglected and in
reality it was much better than had been supposed.   One such
reappraisal appeared in a *Handbook of Canadian Literature* by
Archibald MacMurchy, published at Toronto in 1906.

The author cherishes the hope that this small volume shows
conclusively that the Canadians, though so much engaged in
exploring, surveying, and cultivating the wide territories of
the Dominion, are not one whit behind the gifts of imagination
and fancy to be found in other parts of the world.   The truth
appears to be that the literary production of the people of the
Dominion is proportionately equal, in quantity and quality, to
that of any like part of the English-speaking race.[3]

[1]Klinck, *op. cit.* p. 82; Connor, Carl. Y.: *Archibald Lampman.* Montreal,
1929.   Pp. 91-92.
[2]*A History of Canada.*   Boston, New York, London, 1898.   Pp. 422-423.
[3]MacMurchy, Archibald: *Canadian Literature.* Toronto, 1906.
Pp. iii-iv.

Even stronger was the language used in *Highways of Canadian Literature*, written by Dr. J. D. Logan and Donald French, and first published in 1924:

> . . . the best Canadian poetry and imaginative prose will compare favourably with the admittedly authentic poetry and prose of many of the significant British and United States authors in the mid-Victorian era. In Canadian verse in English are genuine 'gems' of poetry, which, for vision, imagery, passion, lyrical eloquence, verbal music, and mastery of form and technique, are hardly, if at all, surpassed by the poetry of Coleridge, Shelley, Keats, Wordsworth, Tennyson, Swinburne.[1]

And to those who were always harping on Canada's youth, one of our leading literary journalists rejoined sharply, in 1931: "What we are suffering from is not youth but age," and he added: "Canadian literature is a good deal better than is generally admitted. Its low rating is primarily due to the timidity of Canadians, and to their ignorance of the subject . . . Most of the best examples of Canadian literature have never been read by the vast majority of Canadians; a large proportion of the best living Canadian writers could not pass creditably an examination on the outstanding books that have been produced in their own country."[2]

These are stout statements, apt to evoke cheers from many an enthusiastic Canadian, but when the evidence is examined today in a coldly critical spirit, how valid is the conclusion? It is notably difficult to rank living authors; but what of Archibald MacMurchy's confident assertion of 1906? His own *Handbook* offers very little evidence that Canada's literary production up to that date was 'proportionately equal, in quantity and quality, to that of any like part of the English-

[1]Logan, J. D., and French, D. G.: *Highways of Canadian Literature.* Toronto, 1924. P. 16.
[2]*Open House*, edited by William Arthur Deacon and Wilfred Reeves. Ottawa, 1931. P. 304.

speaking race' unless he merely meant that it was no worse than that of Australia, New Zealand or South Africa at the same date. Of the Canadian authors listed in his *Handbook*, covering 150 years of English-language settlement in British North America, there are only three or four who won any sort of international reputation, even in their own day. Haliburton certainly meets the test. But Heavysege was essentially an Englishman writing in Canada on Biblical themes, and can hardly qualify. John Richardson might conceivably be included, though he was little read in 1906, and is almost unknown today. Roberts became internationally known for his animal stories, but his poetry and history had no widespread reputation even in Canada, and even less elsewhere. Who else, up to 1906, could be plausibly included in any compendium of world literature? The long barren period might as well be acknowledged, for it cannot be hidden.

More perceptive studies of Canadian letters have begun to appear in the past quarter of a century. The names of W. E. Collin, E. K. Brown, A. . JM. Smith and the editors of the *University of Toronto Quarterly*'s annual survey of Letters in Canada come to mind. Some new ground was broken by E. K. Brown in his monograph, *On Canadian Poetry*, first published in 1943. In that work, Dr. Brown skilfully disentangled several factors which have retarded Canadian literary production, some with economic, some with psychological or spiritual roots. There is colonialism, the utilitarian spirit of the frontier, and the incubus of an extreme Puritanism. And for me the most illuminating assertions in his whole analysis were these: "Literature develops in close association with society," and "A great literature is the flowering of a great society." He went on to quote the poet E. J. Pratt with telling effect: "The lonely, brooding spirit, generating his own steam in silence and abstraction, is a rare spirit, if indeed he ever existed, and as

far as one may gather from scientific discussions on the point,
there is no biological analogy for this kind of incubation.
Rather, the mountains come to birth out of the foothills, and
the climbing lesser ranges. The occasional instance cited in
literary history of personal isolation ignores the context of spiritual companionship with books and causes and
movements."[1]

Another study of the factors militating against the creation
of a Canadian Literature was made a few years later by
Edward A. McCourt, prairie novelist. In an essay prepared
as one of the studies of the Massey Commission (1951), he
wrote: "The failure of Canadian writers to create a national
literature of much significance to Canada or the rest of the
world has, in the past half-century, been many times analyzed.
Numerous discussions have pointed to four factors as obvious
deterrents to the development of creative writing in this
country. They are the colonial spirit, the Canadian publisher, the Canadian reading public, and the Canadian
critic." McCourt agreed that the colonial spirit had led to
numerous shadowy imitations of English works. He thought,
too, that in trying to throw off colonialism, we have suffered
from another evil—"a petty, self-conscious nationalism which
for the past two decades has tended to dominate too much of
our thinking about the creative arts. The cry 'Be Canadian'
still reverberates around us; but few of our literary critics who
became particularly vocal after the Statute of Westminster
have bothered to explain just what being Canadian in
literature means. Generally, they seem to have associated
the phrase with background; and until recently the writer who
took pains to introduce a maple tree or beaver into his setting
was fairly sure of getting credit marks from some critics,
regardless of the quality of his art."

McCourt then examined the indictment against the

[1]Brown, E. K.: *On Canadian Poetry*. Toronto, 1944. P. 26.

Canadian publisher, whose position, he agreed, was a peculiar and equivocal one. To a large extent the difficulty of the Canadian publisher was the apathy of the Canadian book-buying public. McCourt quoted some angry sentences from an article written by Frederick Philip Grove for the *University of Toronto Quarterly:*

The Canadian public is ignorant, cowardly and snobbish; it is mortally afraid of ideas and considers the discussion of first principles as a betrayal of bad manners.

Unless they are very sure that it is socially disgraceful not to own a given book, they refuse to buy it. If it is imperative, socially, that they are able to talk about it, they borrow it. . . .

More appallingly, Canadians are at bottom not interested in their own country; I honestly believe they prefer to read about lords and dukes, or about the civil war in the United States. They are supposed to be born explorers; but they have not yet heard that the human heart and soul are perhaps the only corners in this universe where unexplored and undiscovered continents are still abounding.[1]

McCourt thought Grove was unfair in implying that the Canadian reading public was any more ignorant, more cowardly, or more snobbish than the reading public of other countries, particularly of the United States. The truth is, McCourt added, "that all reading publics are more or less ignorant and cowardly in the sense that Mr. Grove uses these terms."

McCourt concluded that in view of the unusual difficulties under which they operate, Canadian publishers have done all that can be reasonably expected of them to help Canadian literature, and particularly poetry.

As for the charge that inadequate criticism has failed creative writing in Canada, the Saskatoon novelist and critic observed mildly that "intelligent literary criticism is ordinarily the concomitant of a mature culture; and it has yet to be

[1] *University of Toronto Quarterly*, Vol. VII, No. 4. Pp. 459-460.

shown that lack of it seriously retards literary development. On behalf of the critics it might be argued that since criticism grows by what it feeds on, it is inevitable that in Canada its growth should be somewhat stunted.''

One consoling circumstance for the anxious Canadian, ashamed of the poverty of Canadian letters even after 150 years of settlement, did lie in the indubitable fact that other settlements of European peoples in North America and other extensions overseas had done no better. The English settlements on the Virginia coast began in 1606; the Pilgrim Fathers arrived at Cape Cod in 1620; the Massachusetts Bay Colony dates from 1630. But two centuries yawn between these arrivals and the first authentic literary "flowering" of New England. The literary achievement of New Englanders in those two intervening centuries was no more remarkable than that of the similar years of settlement in British North America. In the English colonies further south, the record was still less impressive. Except for Sidney Lanier, the American South failed for 250 years to produce a single major poet.

G. E. Woodberry, reporting on American Literature in *Chambers Encyclopaedia of English Literature* (1903), offered the view that "the 'slender beginnings' of American literature, in the main written by authors of English birth and published in the mother country, yielded little of even antiquarian memory beyond Roger Williams's *The Bloudy Tenent of Persecution*, Anne Bradstreet's *Poems*, and the *Bay Psalm Book*. Life in the colonies was, indeed, further illustrated by sermons, diaries, letters, and other records either then issued or collected since made accessible by historical societies; but their importance is rather social than literary."

Woodberry added:

The north-eastern colonies, and, in particular, those of New England, were the chief, and, in fact, almost the exclusive

sources of such literature as there was. . . . Of polite literature there was at best only a small product, and that consisted
of the most feeble, awkward, and inane imitation of the
reigning English schools.

Literature in the true sense did not exist in the first two
centuries of life there [the biographer of Poe and Hawthorne
continued]. The printed word was used as a social instrument
with great power, but not for literary ends; it was in the service
of theology, history, government, the practical or pious life;
it was primarily speculative, religious, legal, employed for
discussion and record. There was no literary class, nor any
room for one, in the scheme of life; there was no market for
their works.[1]

All these remarks would apply to a large extent to the early
settlers of the Canadian Provinces. Indeed, the circumstances
in most of British North America were in the main even less
favourable. In several of the American colonies, especially
New England, the people were lettered, the society had schools
and colleges and an educated class; as Woodberry reports,
"it maintained and continued high respect for the intellectual
and scholarly life and the power of the mind." But in spite
of these favourable factors, no body of fine literature of any
importance appeared there for 200 years. Was it likely that
the record of British North America, much of it cut off more
effectively from the mother cultures, would be much better?

Walter C. Bronson, another historian of American literature,
displays considerable bewilderment at the long, long stretch
of literary sterility in the American Colonies and during the
early years of the Republic. In a work published in 1900,
before the new frontier theories of Frederick Jackson Turner
had made much of an impression on American historical
research, Bronson contrasted the literary production of the

[1]P. 731-733.

homeland with that of colonial America. In a mood of
apology and explanation, he wrote:

During the first three-fourths of the seventeenth century,
the period when most of the English colonies in America were
planted, England was the home of great men and of a great
literature. Spenser had died as the old century went out,
Shakespeare and Bacon lived on into the new, and Milton was
born one year after the settlement of Jamestown. The
colonists were of the same stock which had just produced these
and other literary Titans.

Bronson conceded that it would be unreasonable to expect
equally great writers in the forests of America. He cited the
usual reasons for the low level of literary production in the
American colonies, the exactions of the wilderness, the task of
setting up a political state, the relatively small population in
the early years. "Since genuises are rare in every generation,
it is no wonder that they were not numerous among the few
hundred thousand inhabitants scattered along the Atlantic
seaboard. It must be said, however, that not only the great
lights were absent from America, but the lesser ones as well,
and that the general level of literary talent was low." He
thought the character of the colonists might have had something to do with it as well as the unfavourable environment,
mentioning that "among the early settlers of the South were
many paupers, convicts and needy adventurers."
Bronson put forward these and other explanations as
though he himself was not wholly convinced by them.
"During the last quarter of the seventeenth century and the
greater part of the eighteenth, literature in England itself was
comparatively inferior," he goes on, the presumption being
that a similar slump would not be unreasonable across the
Atlantic. Yet his uneasiness at the long barren period
persists. Even in the "age of prose and reason" he noted,
Britain could boast names like Dryden, Addison, Swift, Pope,

Fielding, Gray, Goldsmith, Johnson, Gibbon and Hume—
where were the American counterparts of these? "American
literature," confessed the historian, "for the same period has—
with two exceptions—no names worthy of a place beside
them. A colonial literature," he summed up, "has the
advantage of inheriting the riches of an old civilization; it has
the disadvantage of crude surroundings and lack of originality." Such was the case with American literature for
two hundred years.[1]

The Cambridge *History of American Literature* tells a similar
tale. Of New England verse, the writer observes that it was
as utilitarian and matter of fact as any prose, consisting
largely of narratives of voyages, annals of the colonies,
descriptions of flora, fauna and the scenery, "versified for the
jingle." The most characteristic products of early New
England versifiers were the memorial poems, which at least
met a popular demand. Even less congenial for the development of a native literature were the scattered plantations of
the South. The southern colonists, recalls the Cambridge
History, were not of a literary class.[2] The conditions were
distinctly unfavourable for letters. There were at first no
schools, no printing presses, no literary centres. There were
few who wanted to read, and even fewer who wanted to write.
New York produced practically no English verse until the
Revolution. The Carolinas and Georgia continued barren
until nearly the close of the eighteenth century.

Charles Angoff, in his *Literary History of the American People*,
noted that the Virginians did not settle in groups of families,
like the New Englanders. The play of mind on mind, he said,
so common in Boston, Salem and Hartford, was completely

[1] *American Literature*. Boston, 1919. P. 7.
[2] James Truslow Adams, however, challenges the old tradition of the
continuous literary preeminence of New England, and says that the early
gazettes of Virginia and South Carolina were better in a literary way
than those of New England.

lacking, and the Virginia culture, what there was of it, was
much inferior to that of the Northern Colonies. But even in
the Northern Colonies there was a long literary lag. Vernon
Parrington, in *The Colonial Mind*, after reviewing the
philosophy of the greater minds among the immigrants to New
England, wrote:

With the passing of the emigrant generation, a narrow
provincialism settled upon the Commonwealth of Massachusetts Bay. Not a single notable book appeared; scarcely
a single generous figure emerged from the primitive background. A thin soil and the law of Moses created a capable
but ungainly race, prosaic and niggardly. Their very speech
lost much of the native English beauty that had come down
from mediaeval times. The clean and expressive idiom that
Bunyan caught from the lips of English villagers, with its
echoes of a more spontaneous life before the Puritan middle
class had substituted asceticism for beauty, grew thinner and
more meagre, its bright homespun dyes subdued to a dun
butternut. The town records, which in the first years had
been set down in dignified and adequate phrase, became
increasingly crabbed and illiterate, laboriously composed by
plain men to whom spelling had become a lost art. The
horizons of life in New England were contracting to a narrow
round of chores and sermons.[1]

Some of the English settlements in British North America
began with as likely a stock and as favourable an environment
for literary production as did New England: others in the
interior were under greater handicaps than any settlement
along the Atlantic Coast. If two centuries intervened before
the first era of important creative writing appeared in New
England it was, perhaps, unreasonable to expect very much
great literature from the first 150 years of British North
American settlement.

A similar story of cultural set-back and long delay in the
creation of the fine arts, including *belles lettres*, can be traced in

[1] *Main Currents in American Thought*, Vol. 1, New York, 1927. P. 84.

other colonial histories.   It is sufficient here, perhaps, to note that the greater part of early Australian literature was the work of writers born and bred in Great Britain, that early native writing aped that of the Mother country, and that the first significant literary activities were connected with such vigorous journals as the *Sydney Bulletin*.   The New Zealand story is similar.

The early literature in English in South Africa was severely utilitarian or took the familiar form of the experiences · of missionaries, explorers, hunters and shipwrecked sailors, written by English-born authors who owed nothing to South Africa but a stimulus and a theme.   As for native letters, the introduction to *The Centenary Book of South African Verse* (1925) recites the familiar factors.   Conditions were adverse; the European population scattered over a vast area; pioneer years of storm and strife offering few intervals wherein "to recollect their emotions and cultivate the civilizing art of poetry"; education a luxury which only the children of the well-to-do might enjoy; with a small reading public, professional writers could not be supported; the dregs of time only devoted to literature; a local deterrent the paucity of sound criticism; no good *Reviews;* newspapers immersed in politics and commerce; smaller papers conducted by men not qualified to criticize literary work."[1]

The long cultural lag is indeed characteristic of such frontier extensions of older societies.   Accordingly, it may be supposed that the same general forces were at work everywhere.   The stock explanations for the literary unproductivity of colonies, and for the mediocrity of much early work, do not take us very far toward understanding what these factors are. "The frontier absorbs their energies," say the historians,, with the implication that when the frontiersman gets his wind again, the literary masterpieces will begin to appear.   "The

[1]Slater, F. Carey, London, 1925.   Pp. vii-ix.

population at first is too small"—as though growth of numbers alone will guarantee a supply of native Chaucers and Balzacs. "There is the disadvantage of crude surroundings"—as though a few boulevards and parks, some Wedgewood china and a few reclining chairs, would speed up the appearance of an authentic native literature. Bronson's final explanation, that pioneer peoples lack originality, is even less convincing. Some very original notions and inventions—addressed, it is true, to other phases of human activity—have been produced and promoted in pioneer settlements where a hostile environment had to be subdued. Necessity is the mother of invention. But *belles lettres* were not among the pioneer essentials.

CHAPTER II

CLIMATE AND SOIL IN LITERARY
FLOWERINGS

E. K. Brown's cogent observation, that "literature is the flowering of a society," suggests another approach to Canadian literary history. What kinds of societies have elsewhere flowered into great literature? Is it possible to study the cultural soils and cultural climates and find out which sorts seem to favour the creation of literary works? If certain social, technical and cultural prerequisites are needed for the growth and development of important literatures, and these can be identified, it may be possible to re-examine the transplanting of European cultural life to the North American continent, and consider how long it would take before such favourable circumstances could be reproduced in a new land.

In short, if any working laws or principles can be deduced from a study of older cultures, they might thus be used to illuminate the growth of literature on this side of the Atlantic. Interesting questions suggest themselves. Were the typical conditions of the North American frontier conducive to important literary production? Was the society one from which a great literature was to be expected? What is the minimum of cultural, educational and critical apparatus, what degree of integration of society, what spiritual values, what degree of growth of an interested audience, what market, must precede a literary era? In short, what would be necessary before in North America the environment which supported the great periods of European literary production could be reproduced? Could it be done in fifty, or a hundred, or two hundred years?

Of course, some one may interject, even if immigrants were to succeed in re-creating on North American soil a cultural setting adequate for such a literary bloom, there would be no guarantee that the growth would take place. "Flowerings" need seed as well as climate and soil. This is readily granted, with the observation, however, that even the best seed without soil or climate will not flower either.

So far as I know, even the most profound scholar has not fully accounted for the supreme moments of literary achievement: of Sophoclean Athens, the Italian Renaissance, the England of Elizabeth. There is always an imponderable element:

> The spirit bloweth and is still,
> In mystery our soul abides. . . .

But the more mundane aspects of any recent Golden Age are open for study. There are forerunners, prerequisites, attendant circumstances. Examination of these would, no doubt, point to specific elements in a society without which no material achievement in the field of letters could be expected. A Shakespeare does not appear overnight in a tribe of nomadic herdsmen: he could not be a Shakespeare in such a setting. It is a moot point, as one writer has put it, whether "men produce movements, or movements men." Both may be true. The philosopher, W. E. Hocking, gets at the heart of the matter in the following comment: "In the normal order, one's enjoyment of his own work is at the same time the enjoyment of others' enjoyment of that work; and this enjoyment has a dimension which varies with the numbers his work can reach. The great players produce the great game; but the great game as an occasion does its part in bringing out the great players."[1]

The Golden Ages of Literature were preceded by generations if not centuries of literary pioneering and experimentation: the orchestra, as it were, "tuning up" in preparation for the great symphony. But looking much farther back in history, before a civilization could be created at all, before any of the arts could be invented, a certain measure of economic security must first be won. What we sometimes forget in looking at the colonial settlements of northern North America, is that when the first colonists arrived they were greeted by a virtually untouched wilderness, thinly occupied by New Stone Age peoples, who in some areas had not taken even the first of these steps toward a literate civilization. Nor do we fully appreciate the fact that the North American colonists from Europe had to recapitulate in a few decades the story of progress from the New Stone Age to modern civilization, an evolution which had taken their ancestors around the Mediterranean many thousands of years.

To live in Indian or Eskimo country at all, it might be necessary for a while to go back a very long way in history. "The wilderness," writes F. J. Turner, "masters the colonist. It finds him a European in dress, industries, tools, modes of travel and thought. It takes him from the railroad car and puts him in the birch canoe. It strips off the garments of civilization and arrays him in the hunting shirt and the mocassin. . . . In short, at the frontier, the environment is at first too strong for the man. He must accept the conditions which it furnishes, or perish." When the United Empire

[1]*Man and the State*.   New Haven, 1926.   Pp. 238-239.

Loyalists ascended the Saint John River in 1784, they found the old settlers, the Acadians and Pre-Loyalists "almost as wild as Indians."[1]   Similar observations can be made on any frontier.

If neither the Algonquins nor the Eskimos had found it possible to create on North American soil an advanced and literary culture, the reasons are not far to seek.   Nomadic hunters and fishermen possess few goods.   "Wealth is the prelude to art.   In every country where centuries of physical effort have accumulated the means for luxury and leisure, culture has followed as naturally as vegetation grows in a rich and watered soil.   To have become wealthy was the first necessity: a people must live before it can philosophize."   "All art is the product of leisure," wrote F. P. Grove.   And wealth makes leisure possible.

Or, to go still further back: "The emergence of the Neolithic way of life was perhaps the greatest of many great developments in human progress which originated in the Near East, for it lies at the root of all progress toward civilization.   For hundreds of thousands of years, men had lived a nomadic life in small groups.   It was only with the cultivation of grain and the domestication of animals that settled life became practicable; and only when men had settled down in one place, with reasonable assurance of economic necessities, did they have the leisure to develop arts and crafts."[2]

The aborigines of northern North America were still in the primitive state in which our European ancestors had earlier been living "for hundreds of thousands of years."   The first explorers found them in such a stage; and the early European

---

[1] Turner, Frederick Jackson: *The Frontier in American History*. New York, 1921.   P. 4.   Wright, Esther Clark: *The Loyalists of New Brunswick*. Fredericton, 1955.   P. 219.

[2] See Will Durant, *The Story of Philosophy*. New York, 1927.   P. 577. The reference to neolithic life is from a broadcast over the BBC by Kathleen M. Kenyon, printed in *The Listener*, June 4, 1953.

settlers took over a wilderness in which the savages and barbarians had hunted, fished and fought. It is not suggested that in order to live in that wilderness the European was compelled to revert completely to savagery or barbarism: he had brought along with him many of the cultural tools and heritages of an advanced civilization. Yet, as Turner points out, some regression was inescapable. The wilderness remoulded European man. If all the fine arts, such as *belles lettres*, had to be left behind for a while, what wonder?

Before a Golden Age, or, for that matter, any kind of Age of Polite Letters could be looked for on North American soil, it would be necessary for the colonists and settlers to import or bring into being in a new continent at least some of the cultural and technical equipment and environment which had assisted in all the literary movements of Europe, but which, over there, had required several thousand years of growth and evolution.

What are the barest essentials without which no literary production of any consequence can be expected? An effective demand: a literate and interested audience, to begin with: a substantial body of readers sufficiently well educated to welcome—and reward—the output of the author. Could the first wave of immigrants into a new country supply even this basic requirement? Yet the first generation in the new land would be more literary than the second or third. The first generation of immigrants would inevitably include a few advanced products of the long era of European scholarship: they would read, and perhaps also create minor literary works. But what would the next generation on the new continent be like, raised on a rude frontier? That would depend on the schools, teachers, libraries and periodicals of the new land, as well as on the home influences.

Can such luxuries be provided overnight? One can conceivably picture boatloads of Europeans setting forth for their new North American home bearing in their heads and incorporating into their personalities the accumulated literary wisdom of many millenia: (a fanciful picture at that, if carried very far, because the most useful pioneers might be skilled artisans who had never opened a book since childhood). But how much of the necessary apparatus and equipment of a literary culture could they take with them to the new settlements? And when, seeking new land, the first wave of pioneers left the seacoast (where at least they had intermittent re-contact with the fires of European civilization), and plunged into the trackless forest, how much of that scanty literary apparatus would go with them? They were as likely to transport a grand piano through the pathless swamps as a large library or a printing press. Guns and axes might be the top limit of their impedimenta.

There are two analogies which seem to me to throw light on the process of transferring elements or segments of an old and sophisticated culture to an untamed continent. One is the familiar botanical or ecological parallel: and the other involves the spreading of flame. On the whole the former seems the more applicable. The re-creation on North American soil of a European civilization involved many of the problems faced by any gardener who tears a plant out of its *milieu*, away from its accustomed plant and insect associations, and seeks to persuade it to flourish in an alien setting.

The gardener knows, to begin with, that some stocks will not transplant at all, no matter how much care is taken. That was true, too, of some of the immigrants, misfits, weaklings, who promptly returned or died. Another elementary notion is that plants with vigorous root-stocks, with large self-contained food reserves as in tubers, corms or bulbs, or with ample store of undisturbed soil about the roots, usually thrive better than those without. Colonists who could migrate as a society, and who could take with them the essential implements for life abroad, together with some reserves of food, were more likely to survive and flourish than isolated individuals with no equipment. And finally it is common for all transplants to suffer a shock which may take a long time to overcome: for a while the plants may appear to be dying; they contract and shrivel, and show little evidence of bud development, but if the roots live, and they can hang on for a season or two, they may in due course make a complete adjustment to the new soil and the new setting, and branch out vigorously—even, perhaps, more vigorously in time than they would have done in their old environment.

In the transplanting of human societies, as in plant societies, the nature of the cultural soil to which they are moved is of paramount importance, as are the new climate and other environmental factors. Soil accumulates over the ages, even on the most rocky terrain. It might be possible to keep a bulb alive in sand or on rock for a while, it might even flower for a time, until its reserves were exhausted: but there would be no progeny. I think some of the *émigré* writers in North America were essentially in this fix; they came to this continent in the full bloom of their own literary activity: and they continued for a while to write and produce on North American soil, relying, perhaps on the publishers and presses and reading public of Europe to enable them to reach literary fruition. Ripped out of their ancestral soil, they tended to be lonely and to go into a literary decline. And their sons and daughters born and brought up in North American surroundings did not inherit the literary fire: when the *émigrés* died, the inherited and transported fire largely died with them. They lived, like Heavysege, in a utilitarian commercial society, not yet ready to catch fire from them.

One more parallel before I leave these analogies. Before a distant bonfire of damp wood is well established from the parent flame, repeated contact may be necessary; the first sparks may have to be supplemented, time and again, with new flame from the mother source. Those parts of North America which could most readily maintain a live contact with older transatlantic centres of literary culture had a better chance of establishing a native growth or a self-fed flame, than those permanently cut off from all contact, by pathless forest or vast ranges of rugged hills.

These analogies may help, also, to understand why, as a literary culture was slowly established in North America, it should have appeared when and where it did.

James Truslow Adams, whose studies and reflections threw such valuable light on the pioneer process in the United States, even finds a standard pattern of three stages in the life of pioneer settlements, reminiscent of the botanical transplant: first, "a purely transplanted growth, subject to slow modification and disintegration under the influences of the wilderness. Next the short period of extreme declension and of hesitation succeeding upon the withering of this imported culture, and thirdly the period of development of a native-born one."[1] One might object that the transported European culture never entirely withered, that it was re-moulded and adapted for better North American utilization; but the broad process, much as Adams has described it, can be traced in the story of every North American settlement.

Decades of patient scholarship have by now so thoroughly reconstructed the colonial settlements of New England that all the materials are available for an exhaustive scrutiny of the fate of artistic culture when Europeans cross the Atlantic, set up seaboard establishments, multiply and expand and begin to penetrate the interior. (Much more waits to be done with Canadian material). The wilderness begins its transforming process on the first immigrants, but the more spectacular changes are still to come. As the white man

[1] *Provincial Society.* New York, 1927. P. 258.

pushed west he created a continuous moving frontier, enduring
for nearly three centuries, until at last, the pioneers of, say,
Montana, were sons of the pioneers of Minnesota, who were
sons of the pioneers of Ohio, who were the sons of the pioneers
of New York State, who were the sons of the pioneers of New
Hampshire, and so on.   If the early immigrant on the seaboard is still European man, his children will be more North
American man, and their children in turn will be more and
more the product of the new environment and less and less
indebted to the traditional cultures of Europe.   As Adams
made clear to thousands of readers for the first time, in his
book *The Epic of America*, the rolling wave of migration across
North America sorted and selected and moulded the human
material.

The first frontier of settlement had not really been an
American frontier at all.   All the settlers had England for a
background. . . . As a newer frontier formed at the back of
the old settlements, there was, it is true, no European background, but the pioneers were nowhere far from our oldest
settled country.   To a considerable extent, however, in passing
the population through this second sieve, the learned and
gentle were left behind, and rawness and lack of culture were
increased along the border.   The American population has
been squeezed through such a sieve over and over again, and,
when the first migrations over the mountains occurred, there
was another elimination of education and refinement.   Moreover, with each successive swarming out from the older
settlements the background of culture and beauty became
more and more meagre. . . . Life had been growing freer and
more independent for the poor, but also less cultured in the
broadest sense.   American advance has always involved a
selection.   If that selection has meant that the more democratic, the more independent, courageous and ambitious—as
well, it might not be forgotten, as the more shiftless—have
passed on the frontiers as pioneers, so has it also meant that
those for whom education, the pleasures of social life, aesthetic
and intellectual opportunities of one sort and another have

counted as more important than a material getting ahead, have for the most part usually stayed behind.[1]

When, after several generations, the transforming power of the wild hinterland on the European stock has done its work, and created a new North American, who was certainly not a copy of the Algonquin or Iroquois, because of his European inheritance, but who was no longer a very close copy of the sophisticated urban European either, the subsequent confronting of these two types with each other produced some interesting reactions. The North American frontiersman commonly thought the cultured visitor from overseas useless, snobbish, arrogant and effete; the British or European visitor frequently found the North American ill-mannered, uncouth, ignorant and conceited. The celebrated opinions of Charles Dickens, Mrs. Trollope, Miss Martineau and Captain Marryat about "Yankees" and other Americans were keenly resented, and no wonder, considering what they said.

[1] *The Epic of America.* New York, 1931. Pp. 122-123.

CHAPTER III

THE CULTURAL VALUES OF
THE FRONTIER

No account of the birth and growth of native letters in British North America can be more than a segment of a much larger story, namely, its social and cultural history. North America was settled by migrations from a mature and sophisticated society. These migrations involved uprooting and transplanting. A few small communities may have been transferred substantially *en masse;* but by and large the occupation of North America by peoples of European stock involved first the scattered movement of individuals and families ripped from their ancient European *milieu;* and then the re-creation on North American soil of new societies, composed of the miscellaneous human ingredients, which a mixture of chance and design had brought together in the new land. It may seem like going a long way back to consider the broad nature of such human migrations in an examination of native Canadian letters; but I am convinced that it is a fruitful approach and throws some light on the nature of our literature.

28

There have been human migrations from time immemorial. The fate of migrants in their new setting is always, perhaps, unpredictable, but some rough laws or principles can be discerned, even by the amateur historian. The nature of the societies created in the new land will obviously depend on the character, talents, and personality of the migrants, on the human stock, and on their inherited culture. It will depend, also, on the influences of the new environment. The migrants will be moulded by the geography and economics of their new land. They will also be affected by the new *human* environment into which they are transplanted.

It is quite possible for migrating groups to be swallowed up so completely in their new human setting as to virtually disappear in a few generations. The teeming millions of Central Africa, it seems, have absorbed in this way over the millenia many trickles of humanity from northern regions— from Europe and the Mediterranean and the middle East. Even vestiges of their influence are difficult to trace today. The migration of a few individuals or families into a densely populated area is always, perhaps, likely to end up in such virtually complete assimilation, unless the immigrants are possessed of exceptional social cohesion and spiritual pertinacity.

But the settlement of North America, certainly in the lands north of the Rio Grande, was not an absorption or annihilation of this nature. Amerindian society did not, indeed, possess the power to absorb and remould the European immigrant, except in a few special cases like the *coureur de bois*, or some small communities of the *Métis*. For reasons which it is not necessary to develop here, the migrants to northern North America rejected any such opportunities as there might have been to become a strand in the social fabric of the Algonquin and the Iroquois nations. There was an effective time gap— of several millenia—between the two cultures, and a decisive religious and philosophical barrier.   Moreover, the closely-knit immigrant society soon greatly outnumbered the scattered aborigines.

Indeed, the idea of being absorbed into the aboriginal societies of North America never entered into the minds of the European settlers.   They had the proud consciousness of superiority.   They not only proposed to cling jealously to their European heritage, compounded of Greek and Roman and Hebrew elements and moulded by the Reformation, the Counter Reformation and the Renaissance.   They were determined to re-create on North American soil a civilization similar to that which they had left behind in Europe, with, of course, some of the old weaknesses and evils expunged, and more noble qualities substituted in their stead.   Those who thought about it might well have conceded that the environment of North America would dictate some modifications of European customs and habits.   But the spirit and philosophy of the new North American society was to be European, certainly not Indian, or anything else.

In these aims and aspirations, the new settlers were not, as it proved, seriously frustrated.   They *did* re-create on North American soil a civilization with basic similarities to that which had been built up in Europe.   It could not be exactly the same, because on the one hand the obstacles, and on the other hand the superior potentialities, affected for worse or better their prospects of doing so.   But it was a true extension, an organic outgrowth of Western European culture, not in any material sense a reversion to the New Stone Age culture of the North American Indian.

Among the institutions and heritages which the European immigrants brought across the Atlantic were, of course, the arts of writing and reading, and an awareness of the world of polite letters, even among those never likely to dabble in it. It was reasonable to expect that in due course the colonists would foster on North American soil all the intellectual, aesthetic and technical activities which would make likely the emergence of a native literature along the lines of western European tradition.

The process by which individuals, families and segments of societies are uprooted, are transferred, go pioneering on virgin soil, and in due course construct new societies in new lands, is a large theme in North American frontier history. Much of the process was completed in the seventeenth, eighteenth and nineteenth centuries, but it is still occurring today. Many living Canadians have witnessed pioneer development from its beginning, many witness it today. When, for example, my father guided his walking plow across our Alberta homestead fifty miles south of Medicine Hat, his plowshare broke virgin sod. My brother and sister and I attended the very first classes ever held in the little white schoolhouse across the open Hudson's Bay section. When a few devout worshippers gathered in our modest frame farmhouse one summer Sunday, it was the very first time Christian service had ever been celebrated within an area as large as an English county. The society which grew up around us was a true pioneer society, constituting the first wave of European or western culture impinging on an unoccupied area, just taken over from the Blackfeet Indian, the coyote and the bison. And, of course, on the advancing edge of frontier settlement in various parts of Canada this process continues.

Among such settlements as were built up in the central and northern part of North America by European migration, what were the prospects for a continuation, or, if that was not possible, the early resumption (after a setback), of such cultural activities as the writing and publishing of polite letters? A few American colonies were planned, but most of them came into being as a combined result of design and chance. But let fancy have free rein for a moment. In the unlikely supposition that an imaginary director of American colonization should have placed high among his priorities the stimulation of native letters in America at the earliest possible moment, what steps could he have taken to ensure such a development?   Could the whole literary complex of a European society be moved entire, *en masse;* that is to say, the reading public, the educational apparatus, the libraries, the printing presses, the publishers, the bookshops, the newspapers, the magazines, the critics?   The absurdity of such a proposal is at once apparent, when one recalls early Atlantic transport and the physical conditions facing the first settlers along the St. Lawrence, on the coasts of New England and Virginia. But without such a "holus-bolus" transplanting of a full-fledged literate society, eager for literary outpourings, would it not be most unlikely that the new settlements would shine as producers of *belles lettres?*

A gradual resumption, on North American soil, of the writing and reading habits characteristic of at least a section of European society might be expected to occur, however, especially under certain types of favourable circumstances. This would provide in time the seedbed for a native North American literature.

The nature of the migrating stock—their traditions, values, ideals—would have an important bearing.   The settlers in some regions *might* include a strong nucleus of literary and intellectual folk, for whom the book was virtually divine, or in any event almost as much a necessity as daily bread and drink.   Some modest literary apparatus and personnel could be carried across the ocean, small libraries and a few printing presses, some scholars to found colleges, some editors to produce periodicals.   This sort of literary flame could be carried over the ocean even in small sailing vessels.   The families and immediate societies of these literary and scholarly folk might then provide a focus or hearth in the new wilderness within which such lore and passion might be kept alive pending more favourable conditions as the settlement grew in wealth and leisure. How successfully such transferred flame could be kept alight would depend largely on the speed and effectiveness with which cultural links could be forged and maintained with the sources of origin. Obviously it would be easier to feed such cultural flame along the Atlantic seaboard or on the shores of the great rivers than in the hinterland, behind the mountains or marshes, certainly until such time as land transportation across North America was improved.

The prerequisites for creating literary works, and those for disseminating them to a wider public are two quite different matters. It seems to me that in theory as well as practice, the conceiving and composition of poetry, essays, fiction and drama could well take place in a colonial settlement long before the social conditions encouraged or indeed permitted the second stage, that of publication and distribution. As against this, the second stage must await the creation of a complex society and an active industry. The conception and creation might be undertaken by immigrant authors, and the publication and distribution of their works might in that event be possible through employment of the established literary apparatus of the mother countries. Then among the second and third generation of the immigrants in the new land, within the family "cell" or scholastic or artistic community in favourable locations, a few writers might appear capable of creating attractive works of a native kind. These too might reach a public through the presses and other facilities of the mother land, North American facilities still being absent or inadequate.

This stage would still, however, fall short in all probability of the makings of a robust and substantial native literature. That would be quite unlikely to appear until the settlements and societies of the new land had matured to the point of

fostering and creating *all* the requirements and appur-
tenances—the substantial reading public, the printing industries, enterprising publishers, booksellers and literary critics.
One could have forecast—and this theory is supported by the
evidence—that the earliest stage of a new country's letters
would see the *émigré* and "tourist" author dominating an
otherwise barren literary landscape. In the next stage the
native writer would appear, struggling to create a native
literature without much help in the way of a native literary
and scholarly community, compelled to rely unduly upon
overseas facilities and support. Finally the day would come
when North American society had matured to the point at
which a native literature would be adequately supported by
and within the society itself. All these stages can be traced
in North American letters, as for example in the two centuries
between the landing of the Pilgrims and the Flowering of
New England.

If literature be indeed a flowering of a society, it is by no
means the only possible flowering. Indeed, the flowers of
society have been almost infinite in variety, and in many ages
and in many parts of the world the printed book has not
appeared at all or has found a very limited place. Which
flowers will germinate and flourish and which will never
appear depends on the seed and on the climate and the
cultural soil.

The smallest unit of society is the family. In the breeding
of the artist it may well be the decisive unit. The spiritual
drive and subsequent career of the incipient writer may have
been essentially fixed and settled before the child moves out
into the larger community surrounding his home. Some
consideration of the pioneer family in North America would
seem to be called for.

The typical pioneer society certainly "flowered" in its own
way, producing men and women who carried on the traditions

of their forefathers, who fought and utilized their environment, and who laid the foundations for the society of today. Why this flowering seldom resulted in the production of literary artists has been hinted at in earlier pages, but deserves further development. It is a theme that has attracted several students of North American life.

Edward J. O'Brien, best known for his collections of short stories, puts the matter very well in an article published in book form in 1935:

Pioneer life is unpropitious to outstanding literary merit. Poe and Herman Melville, for example, are classical examples of what happens to a writer of great individual genius in a frontier civilization. Pioneers have no sympathy to waste on artists. They follow the law of the tribe. In such a society, the artist is expected to be one of the tribe in everything, or he will find himself cut off from the tribe by reason of its instinct for protective solidarity against the perils of the new and strange. The pioneer's partial regression to the primitive is a necessary condition of his survival, and primitive life, as any anthropologist will tell you, is a network of imperatives conceived as taboos.[1]

A somewhat closer scrutiny of the family and clan influences which play upon and mould the growing child in any land will, I think, clarify the central idea of this book. The process is not easily described, because it involves the whole interplay of inheritance and environment, of which we still know very little. But we can start from two reasonably solid assumptions, that potentiality must be present, otherwise there can be no development; and that, given potentiality, the bent of the child will respond sensitively to the early environment.

I have not been able to find a scientific analysis of these factors as they might apply to literary artists of North America. But studies by Amram Scheinfeld have been published in a

[1] *What Is a Book?*, edited by Dale Warren. New York, 1935. P. 168.

related field, that of musical talent. I believe the analogy is close enough to be useful. The great literary artist, like the great musician, is the product of inherited talent plus extensive training. Some years ago a group of outstanding musicians was asked the question: "Which is more important in musical achievement, inherited talent or training?" Most musicians said both were equally important; none dismissed training as unimportant. The same study brought out in detail a fact generally known for a long time, that many if not most of the outstanding musicians of this century came from musical families and out of a musical environment enveloping the family.[1]

A cursory survey of musical biography certainly strengthens the conviction that musicians tend to come out of musical families, or, if not musical families, then musical communities. I suspect, indeed, that only a very small and unimpressive list of outstanding musicians could be compiled who had come from both a non-musical family and a non-musical neighbourhood.

So far as musical performance is concerned, it is rare to find a virtuoso who did not enter upon the practice of music at a very tender age. In the study already cited, the average age when thirty-six virtuosi instrumental artists showed first evidence of talent was four and three-quarter years. Intensive training followed. The inference certainly appears that if the gift had not been recognized, if musical instruments had not been available, if effective teaching had not been undertaken, later achievement would have been lessened, or retarded, or lost entirely. A Franz Liszt might have been born at Fort Edmonton in the early nineteenth century, for example, but it is certain that in that environment he would have been far more likely to end up as a fur-trader or Hudson's Bay clerk than as the outstanding piano virtuoso of his time.

[1] *You and Heredity.* New York, 1939. Pp. 234 *et seq.*

To clinch the point about musical families and societies, a few illustrations may be useful. Liszt's father was a good amateur musician and his first teacher; Franz Schubert "had the advantage of being a member of an intensely musical family, whose string quartet playing was renowned in their suburb." Beethoven's father and grandfather were professional musicians. Brahms was the son of a double-bass player. Mozart's father was a gifted and cultured musician. Richard Strauss was born into a musical circle. Stravinsky's father was an opera singer. Rossini's mother was an opera singer: his father a trumpeter. Smetana's father was a keen amateur musician. Elgar's father was an organist and music-seller. Gounod's mother was a fine pianist. Grieg's mother was a fine pianist and his first teacher. Sterndale Bennett's father and grandfather were professional musicians. The famous Bach family was actively musical for seven generations, of which Johann Sebastian was a member of the fifth. The great-grandfather, the grandfather and the father of Gustav Holst were professional musicians, and his daughter is composer and conductor. There were five generations of musicians in the Couperin family; and there are plenty of other illustrations. A similar study could be made of the larger societies and schools out of which many of the outstanding musicians of Europe came.

The decisive influence of early cultural and spiritual "climate" in a child's development is an old story. "Just as the twig is bent the tree's inclined." Whether any particular home will rear a scholar or a frontiersman, a spendthrift or a miser, a snob or a saint, a rebel or a reactionary, will depend to some extent, certainly, on inheritance, but as much or more on environment. Granted that there is a great range in inherited potentiality, any normal child at birth contains within himself far more possibilities than can ever be realized. What he or she becomes depends largely on what is rewarded and punished in his social group, notably his family circle. This choice between frontiersman and clerk, between cowboy and garage mechanic, between nomadic hunter and solid businessman, is elected for the most part in the earliest years. Usually the range of choice is limited by the environment, but if we are to believe the biologists, the theoretical possibilities are almost unbounded.

"At the beginning of life," writes Alexis Carrel, "man is endowed with vast potentialities. He is limited in his development only by the extensible frontiers of his ancestral predispositions. But at each instant he has to make a choice. And each choice throws into nothingness one of his potentialities. He has of necessity to select one of the several roads open to the wanderings of his existence, to the exclusion of all others. Thus, he deprives himself of seeing the countries wherein he could have travelled along the other roads. In our infancy we carry within ourselves numerous virtual beings who die one by one. In our old age, we are surrounded by an escort of those we could have been, of all our aborted potentialities."[1]

Whether the boy will be a Kit Carson or an Aldous Huxley is certainly decided by hereditary factors in part, but in part also by the influences that play about him in his babyhood and boyhood. The climate of spiritual values is an intangible factor, and very difficult to observe or measure. But there is one field of human growth in which it is possible to see Alexis Carrel's process of irrevocable choice at work in a clear-cut and impressive way. That is in the manner by which the child learns the language of its home, and its country. Why does an English child learn the English language, and a Chinese baby learn Chinese? Is it a matter of physiological endowment? Not at all. It is Carrel's process at work, in

[1] *Man the Unknown.* London, 1936. P. 181.

the fixation of certain habits and the gradual loss of other potentialities.

It is worth while to consider the process involved. The normal baby, soon after birth, is capable of making a vast range of babblings, grunts, hissings—lallations as they are sometimes called—in which presumably the raw stuff or vocal elements of any language used anywhere are there to be detected by a sharp observer. The normal baby is often to be heard in these random and experimental sound effects. Some of them will be encouraged, and "fixed." Others will be ignored and will be neglected and finally lost.

What is noticed and honoured and rewarded will be soon noted by the child, and repeated. The accidental stumbling upon "ma" and "da" sounds, so easy and natural to make, is likely to be greeted with great enthusiasm by the parents; and the normal baby is bright enough to see that he or she has thus made a palpable hit. If such a feat amuses the parents and siblings, if it wins attention, by all means humour them with more of it! In addition, the child learns how to imitate and mimic, and begins to reproduce the English or Swedish or Chinese sounds and combinations which it hears constantly. Its preoccupation with these meaningful sounds tends to reduce the random babblings of the earliest months; and in due course the raw stuff of other languages, the nasalities, glottal clicks, sing-song ululations and so forth die out and cannot ever afterwards be thoroughly mastered. The potentialities in this field, some physiologists tell us, are fairly well settled by the time the child is four or five or six. What is true of skills may be true of values. It may well be that certain spiritual priorities of values, factors in deciding what the mainsprings of adult life will be, have also been settled by that age.

Now we come to the question which is central to this study: what are the conditions within the typical pioneer home, what is the state of the immediate society outside of that home; and are these conducive to the formation of literary craftsmen? What sort of changes in the general frontier society must take place before any considerable group or school of writers and scholars is likely to emerge?

The pre-occupations of the typical pioneer family have been noted. The first stage is usually a stern struggle for survival. Food is vital; shelter, and fuel, in colder climates, are imperative; clothing is hardly less important in the harsher regions and more inclement seasons. In that order, the energies and ingenuities of all the members of the family for a while are thoroughly engaged. If the family must live off the land, a very high premium is at once placed upon the skills of the hunter and the fisherman, and on natural lore prescribing which berries, roots, mushrooms are edible and which poisonous. The patient skilful gardener may stand between the family and the ogre of starvation. If exploration is necessary, as for hunting, ability to find one's way in the wilderness may be a matter of life and death. If trees must be cleared to make land for planting, brawn is invaluable, and so is skill in the use of the axe, in the handling of oxen, or in the use of blasting powder. Logs and boards and shakes are needed for shelter: the axeman and the sawyer are the heroes at this stage. If a pioneer boy wants honour and reward, he will seek to surpass his fellows in fishing, or tracking game, or bringing back more venison for a lower expenditure of precious powder and shot.

The hero of the frontier is the one who can contribute most to the mastery of the adverse environment, whether it be the giant who can clear more land than anyone else about, or later the politician who can get aid from the distant capital for the building and mending of roads. Book learning may be forced to take a back seat for a while, even if the immigrant parents were passionately fond of 'Robbie' Burns or still cling tenaciously to a daily reading of the Good Book.   Even when the first stages of pioneer life are past, and settled communities grow up with villages and towns, the figures who will be honoured and rewarded are much more likely to be the wheelwright, the miller, the veterinarian, the stock-breeder or the merchant, than anyone dabbling in the fine arts.

The way these frontier attitudes persisted into later generations will be illustrated, in later chapters, from Canadian literary history.   The same, of course, was true in American territory.   Hamlin Garland recalled, in *A Daughter of the Middle Border*, the reaction of hard-headed neighbours and farm relatives in Wisconsin to his writing career.   "In truth," he wrote, "little of New England's regard for authorship existed in the valley, and my head possessed no literary aureole.   The fact that I could—and did—send away bundles of manuscript and get in return perfectly good cheques for them was a miracle of doubtful value to my relatives as well as to my neighbours. . . .   Some said, 'I can't understand how Hamlin makes all his money.' . . .   Something unaccountable lay in the scheme of my life.   It was illogical, if not actually illegal."[1]

"If the individual is born and reared in a frontier culture where life is hard and hazardous, where a keen eye and a quick trigger are prized, where hard drinking and harder fighting are manly virtues, and where a square dance to a squeaky fiddle is the highest form of art, he is not likely to achieve fame as a poet, composer, sculptor, philosopher or scientist," writes Leslie A. White in *The Science of Culture*.   White quotes a U.S. sociologist to the effect that 'it is as difficult for an American brought up in the western part of our country (in 1897) to become a good painter as it is for a Parisian to become a good baseball player, and for similar reasons.'   White adds that "the production and incidence of

[1] *A Daughter of the Middle Border*.   London, 1921.   Pp. 101-102, 155.

genius . . . are functions of the cultural setting.   Whether a genius is realized or not depends on the soil and climate of the cultural habitat."[1]

Frontiers move on, and what was once the pioneer fringe becomes old settled country.   The more fortunate locations become prosperous ports, thriving commercial towns, rich stretches of farmland, or university cities.   The acute era of capital formation when frugality and material productivity were the highest virtues may be succeeded by easier and more capacious times.   Wealth may accumulate.   Leisure may become possible.   The people may turn to satisfy some of their spiritual and artistic cravings, long neglected or starved. There may be a renewed zest for contact with the old cultural matrix across the seas, cultural pilgrimages to the fountains of European scholarship and art.   In ways thoroughly familiar to all brought up in pioneer lands, there may reappear a passion for schooling and art and culture as a reaction against the forced crudities of the frontier.   Over the decades the seedbed may be prepared for an artistic flowering.   It may take two hundred years, as it did in New England, but the flowering when it arrives may be a momentous one.

[1] *The Science of Culture.*   New York, 1949.   P. 218.

CHAPTER IV

_____

PRELUDES TO THE NEW ENGLAND
FLOWERING

IN THE PAGES OF James Truslow Adams, Van Wyck Brooks,
Vernon Parrington, Carl Van Doren and others, you can see
the social and cultural seedbed of the American Colonies
(and later the Republic) being readied for such manifestations
as the Boston-Cambridge-Salem-Concord cluster of writers,
and the Literary Flowering of New England.[1]

It took a long time. The cultural setback on the "stern
and rock-bound coast" was severe. So far from showing
cultural progress, there was for the first eighty or ninety years
of settlement all the appearance of a withering of culture.
Adams singles out the decade 1700-1710 as marking the lowest
period of English culture reached before or since.

Let us look at the state of the New England colonies about

[1]Brooks, Van Wyck: *The Flowering of New England.* New York, 1936
(to which I am particularly indebted here); Parrington, Vernon Louis:
The Colonial Mind. New York, 1927; *The Romantic Revolution in America.*
New York, 1927; Wertenbaker, Thomas Jefferson: *The First Americans.*
New York, 1927; Adams, James Truslow: *Provincial Society,* 1690-1763.
New York, 1927; *The Founding of New England.* Boston, 1927; Van Doren,
Carl: *Benjamin Franklin.* New York, 1938, etc.

1700. The Pilgrim Fathers had landed in 1620 and the Massachusetts Bay colony was established in 1630. By 1700 there were reckoned to be 143,000 settlers in the colonies northward from Pennsylvania. But in all that region only forty or fifty boys (attending Harvard) were receiving any education higher than the grammar grades taught in a few schools elsewhere. In the whole territory now within the boundaries of Maine there was not a single school. In 1698, only one child in seventy at Natick, Mass., could read. The only links between most communities were rough trails. Small coastal vessels operated uncertainly, without benefit of aids to navigation. Postal service had begun in 1689 but was not extended until long afterwards. To send a letter from New York to Philadelphia cost nine pence; from Philadelphia to Boston twenty-one pence—the equivalent of at least one dollar and fifty cents today. Without even stagecoach roads, a common intellectual life was impossible. The first attempt to publish a newspaper in 1690 was defeated by this lack of contact with potential subscribers. The Boston *News-Letter* of 1704 was "a pitifully small and dull weekly," which didn't afford even the slightest opening for literary talent.

A quarter of a century later, progress began to be evident. As communications improved, a true society or community could be developed. Almost overnight voluntary clubs and associations began to spring up. The periodical press flourished when the postal service improved. Between 1713 and 1745 no fewer than twenty-two publications were started. Benjamin Franklin and his brother were pioneers in this field.

Printing, the appearance of periodicals in which aspiring authors could try their wings, the development of printshops and binderies capable of issuing native works—all these are so germane to the birth of a native literature that the progress of printing in the American colonies is especially significant. Before 1700, there is very little to relate.

Virginia saw its first press in 1680, seventy-three years after the first settlement, but the printer in charge was ordered to close his establishment for operating without a licence. It seems likely that not a single real book was produced there before the end of the century. In Massachusetts, the first printing press was set up in 1639, and by the end of the century a very respectable number of titles could be reported from Boston, but they were almost exclusively ecclesiastical or political in nature, or of a strictly utilitarian type. *Belles lettres* were rare or non-existent.

This emphasis on useful works, really outside the pale of what we usually call literature, continued for a long time. Carl Van Doren gives a detailed account of the early titles of Benjamin Franklin, who ranks as Philadelphia's second printer. The pioneer, Samuel Keimer, for whom Franklin had worked for a time, brought out in 1728 a folio history of the Quakers, said to be the most important book published up to that time in Pennsylvania, and in 1729 an Epictetus, the first American translation of a classic author. Franklin began his career as printer in the same year with a pamphlet on paper currency. He followed this with Isaac Watts's Psalms and a German hymnbook. Early Franklin titles included almanacs, family doctor books, *The Gentleman's Farrier*, etc. In 1744 Franklin printed Richardson's *Pamela*, said to be the first novel printed in America. This was an exception. "Nine-tenths of what Franklin printed, outside of his official printing of legislative records, laws, treaties, his newspaper and his almanacs, was theological and ephemeral," Carl Van Doren says.

One could make out a convincing case for the assertation that in one way or another Franklin helped along the cause of American letters, directly or indirectly, more than any other man. Franklin's newspaper, the *Pennsylvania Gazette*, became in Adams's view "the most important and entertaining journal" in America. Franklin financed journals elsewhere, and influenced still others. The magazine which he started in 1741 was the most interesting effort to launch a monthly publication. As deputy postmaster general from 1753 on he speeded up the mails. His invention of the Franklin stove, together with the introduction of new lamps from 1750 on, must, Adams thinks, have greatly increased the number of winter-evening readers.

The club was another factor favouring the quickening of social and cultural life and here again Franklin was a pioneer. His "Junto," which first met in 1727, was not narrowly a literary club but it stimulated the intellectual and literary life of Philadelphia, and some of publisher Franklin's early titles were written by members of it.

Franklin saw the connection between wealth, leisure and the arts. In his "Proposal of 1743 for Promoting Useful Knowledge among the British Plantations in America" he asserted that "the first drudgery of settling new colonies, which confines the attention of people to mere necessaries, is now pretty well over; and there are many in every province in circumstances, that set them at ease, and afford leisure to cultivate the finer arts, and improve the common stock of knowledge."[1]

The seedbed was, in fact, being got ready, and the first literary seedlings were soon to appear. The Revolution in some respects greatly retarded, but in others paved the way, for a literary emanation of great brilliance. The eighteenth century saw a rapid increase in the *quantity* of literary output. But it was not until after 1800 that the first internationally famous American authors appeared, in the persons of Washington Irving and Fenimore Cooper.

It is, however, New England in general, and Boston in

[1]Quoted by James Truslow Adams on p. v of *Provincial Society* listed above.

particular, with which we are principally concerned. Here, after 1800, the forerunners and heralds of a literary awakening were increasingly apparent. All the phenomena with which we have come to associate a "Golden Age" of letters were congregating: an accumulation of wealth and the possibility of leisure and travel, a revival of zeal for education and erudition, the launching of literary magazines, the appearance of one or two outstanding teachers, the creation of clubs and cultural societies, and the enlargement of the literary market to the point where professional men and women of letters might subsist and even flourish. As important as the financial rewards were the prizes of prestige and esteem.

Van Wyck Brooks documents the events leading up to Emerson, Prescott, Hawthorne, Longfellow and others. He notes the first theatre in Boston, 1793, the Library of Law, 1806, the Theological Library, 1807, the Boston Athenaeum, 1806, the Handel and Haydn Society, 1815, the Anthology Society of 1803-1812, and the *North American Review* in 1815.

The monthly *Anthology* was the first review of its kind in the country: its members hoped it might foster the growth of a national literature. The soil out of which these institutions sprang was obviously becoming fertile: Boston accumulated great wealth from trade and industry, even benefitting from the war of 1812-1815. In every house, says Brooks, one found the standard authors, Hume, Gibbon, Shakespeare, Milton. Young men went to sea and came back with tales of far-away lands fit to quicken the imagination. Boston corresponded to Plato's city, its population not too large to hear the voice of a single orator. Intellectual life grew apace. The new Argand lamp, improved by Jefferson, had furthered the habit of reading. Cambridge fathers and mothers respected poetry: even wished their boys to be poets. The New England statesmen were also scholars, most of them alumni of Harvard. Learning in Cambridge was immemorial and omnipresent, says Brooks. Everyone there was precocious, and only a dunce could fail to be ready for college at fourteen or fifteen. This was a vast improvement in a century. Harvard had known days of somnolence and scholastic mediocrity, but there had come a renaissance.

In the field of writing and rhetoric, the story of Edward Tyrell Channing of Harvard stands out vividly. He has been obscured perhaps by the reputation of his older brother, Dr. William Ellery Channing, and his uncle of the same name, poet and preacher respectively. You will look for Edward Tyrell Channing in vain in some encyclopaedias, but it could be argued that he was the most important of all the Channings. Consider some of his students and their literary style: Henry David Thoreau, Ralph Waldo Emerson, Richard Henry Dana, John Lothrop Motley, Francis Parkman, Oliver Wendell Holmes. Was it just accident or coincidence that these men who wrote so superbly should all have attended his classes in rhetoric, and written exercises for him at Harvard?

Evidently the learning of other lands and other ages played a prominent part in sparking the literary life of New England. Beginning in 1815, scholars like George Ticknor, Edward Everett and Joseph Green Cogswell surveyed the fruits of European scholarship and brought the modern literature of Europe to the attention of Harvard and other centres of New England culture. Ticknor's father was a rich merchant with a literary bent, and some of his accumulated wealth was laid out in valuable collections of books ransacked out of Europe by his son, who built up the "amplest private library in Cambridge." Archives in many lands were plundered to make possible such works as Prescott's *The Conquest of Mexico*. And as far away as Burlington, Vermont, a lawyer-scholar named George Perkins built up the most complete library of

Scandinavian books in the world, outside the Scandinavian countries.

The literary club also figured in the awakening. Sometimes it took the informal guise of a bookshop operated by a literary enthusiast, man or woman. Ticknor's reading club, organized before 1815, included that incomparable teacher of rhetoric, Edward Tyrell Channing. Prescott was for twenty years member of a literary club. The Peabody bookshop was noted as a place of intellectual stimulation: it was "the liveliest spot" in Boston. It gave birth to *The Dial*. Longfellow founded a Dante Club at Harvard. Another bookstore-club, the Old Corner Bookstore of James T. Fields, contributed to the birth of the *Atlantic Monthly*. The Athenaeum was another fruitful institution. At the peak of New England intellectual and literary fervour there was a vigorous burgeoning of lyceums, lecture societies, libraries and cultural institutes of various kinds.

Finally it should be noted that there was an all-pervasive sense of destiny and purpose, a passionate interest in self-culture. Van Wyck Brooks notes a widely spread presentiment that a great native literature was about to make its appearance. Boston felt appointed to lead the civilization of North America. Hundreds, he said, issued the summons for a literature that was really American, "redolent of the soil." In Boston, as in Florence four hundred years earlier, there was a morning freshness. Young writers were encouraged by their parents in the way the sons of Catholics in some countries were encouraged to become priests. At one stage, everybody in Cambridge seemed to be writing a book. Vehicles for expression sprang up everywhere. One student, says Van Wyck Brooks, counted 137 periodicals of a literary nature established within two decades of the War of 1812-1815. There was a chain of influence. Teachers like E. T. Channing and George Ticknor inspired Emerson, and Emerson in turn inspired hundreds of others.

This, then, was the general atmosphere or climate in which the most notable flowering of North American letters took place. Such a soil and such a climate produced enduring literature. A consideration of the flowering of New England may help to explain why no parallel outburst took place on Canadian soil. It may also help to account for such lesser flowerings of literary works as can be traced in the history of Canadian letters.

CHAPTER V

THE FIRST HARVEST

THE FIRST NATIVE LITERATURE of any consequence
in British North America appeared during the third decade
of the nineteenth century. In 1825, *The Rising Village*, by the
Canadian Oliver Goldsmith, was published in London. In
1828, Joseph Howe purchased the *Novascotian*, of Halifax,
which he proceeded to make into the ablest journal in the
British Provinces. In the following year, the publisher of the
Novascotian brought out a *History of Nova Scotia*, by Thomas
Chandler Haliburton. This was followed six years later
by the first of the Sam Slick papers, which in book form
became the first literary work of international and enduring
reputation to appear in British North America.

This literary flowering of Nova Scotia seems like a precocious achievement for a Province so recently established.
Having in mind that as late as 1784 the population was less
than 40,000, this "creative moment"—as A. G. Bailey aptly
calls it—of which the Howe-Haliburton association was the
crowning glory, came surprisingly soon. The studies of James
Truslow Adams on the New England frontier emphasize the

severe setback to cultural life to be expected among the first
generations. Adams, it will be recalled, fixed 1700-1710 as
marking the cultural low ebb of a region first settled by the
Pilgrims in 1620. More than a century longer was required
to prepare the literary soil and climate for the Flowering of
New England. It is true that when it did arrive it far out-
shadowed the best that Halifax and Windsor could show
in the 1830's. Nevertheless it seems to me quite a remarkable
thing that less than two generations elapsed between the
coming of the Loyalists to Nova Scotia and the maturing of a
literary movement of these dimensions.

The rapidity with which the society of Nova Scotia overcame the shocks of transplanting, and reached a dynamic
condition capable of supporting the literary and cultural
works of the 1820-1840 era can, I think, be explained within
the framework of the frontier thesis examined in the earlier
chapters. The founding of Nova Scotia differed in important
respects from some seaboard communities farther south, and
from all of the hinterland frontiers of North America. Some
of the factors of difference materially favoured the early
appearance of a literary society.

The chief of these factors should be listed.

The immigrant stock of Nova Scotia, especially the Loyalist
migration, was comparatively rich in professional people.

The disruptive effect of migration was lessened in some areas
by the wholesale or *en masse* transfer of families and communities, to a degree less marked in earlier migrations across
the Atlantic.

The movement of the Pre-Loyalists and Loyalists from the
American colonies to Nova Scotia constituted a less destructive
move in social and cultural terms than the longer move from
Europe. The drastic re-moulding by which European man
is made over into American man, using F. J. Turner's language, had already taken place among the Yankee stock of

several generations which moved into Nova Scotia between 1760 and 1790. The migrants adapted themselves to the Nova Scotian setting much more rapidly and completely than Europeans or Britishers could, just as the American home-steaders from Dakota and Iowa took to the Canadian prairies early in this century.

The distances being shorter, and the destinations mainly on the seaboard, a larger amount of cultural paraphernalia could be carried with them. Libraries and printing presses, for example.

The settlements on tidewater in Nova Scotia could, on the whole, maintain better inter-community connections than those among the bush settlers of the hinterland frontier. Even more important, Nova Scotia's position as virtually an Atlantic Island, and the development of coastal and oceanic shipping, made it possible for the settled portions of the new Province to maintain active and frequent links with such stimulating centres of English-language culture as London, New York and Boston.

Some of the natural resources of coastal Nova Scotia could be more quickly and thoroughly exploited than those of the interior forests or plains, some of which had to await modern transportation before they could be developed at all. In this connection, the pioneer work done by the Acadians between 1700 and 1755 in the rich tidal marshlands, the hay meadows and grainlands of the Bay of Fundy should not be ignored. The Windsor area, for example, was already several genera-tions removed from the raw frontier by the time the Pre-Loyalists came in on the invitation of Governor Lawrence in 1760. Thus a third-generation settler of the original New England frontier might be a victim of the "low-ebb" of literary achievement; but a third-generation settler of the Pre-Loyalist migration to the Basin of Minas could be a Thomas Chandler Haliburton.

How large a factor was the first-named, the presence among the Loyalists of a substantial nucleus of professional people, college graduates and other literary folk? The available evidence contains conflicting elements. Earlier writers about the Loyalist tradition made much of this heritage. For example, Charles G. D. Roberts, himself of Loyalist descent on his mother's side, wrote, in his *A History of Canada:*

It is but truth to say that the United Empire Loyalists were the makers of Canada. They brought to our making about thirty thousand people, of the choicest stock the colonies could boast. They were an army of leaders, for it was the loftiest heads which attracted the hate of the revolutionists. The most influential judges, the most distinguished lawyers, the most capable and prominent physicians, the most highly educated of the clergy, the members of council of the various colonies, the Crown officials, people of culture and social distinction—these, with the faithful few whose fortunes followed theirs, were the Loyalists.[1]

But another descendent of the Loyalists, Esther Clark Wright, has more recently examined what she calls the "current notion" that the New Brunswick loyalists came mostly from Massachusetts, that they belonged to the first families of that colony, and that many of them were Harvard graduates. In a study based on original records she found that ninety per cent of them were indeed American born, but only a little over six per cent were from Massachusetts. She added that: "Examination of the occupations of the new-comers dispels the illusion that New Brunswick Loyalists belonged to the first families and were predominatingly Harvard graduates. The number of graduates of all colleges . . . was insignificant in comparison with any one of such trades as carpenters, smiths, cordwainers, tailors, masons or weavers." There were, of course, many farmers.[2]

[1] P. 195.
[2] *Op. cit.* P. 160.

Ray Palmer Baker, however, develops in circumstantial detail the background of the Loyalist stock which settled Nova Scotia, and from him a different impression is received:

> In Nova Scotia at least the refugees represented the highest traditions of American culture. With two hundred graduates of Harvard who removed to the Maritime Provinces were large contingents from younger institutions. . . . At the close of the Revolution over one hundred thousand citizens of the Old Colonies took refuge in British territory—in Nova Scotia, in Canada, in the West Indies, or in Great Britain. . . . John Adams who had no reason to exaggerate, estimated that over "one-third of the influential characters" joined in the exodus. It included, of course, all those who had taken an active part against Congress.[1]

The pioneer soil and climate which are to nourish literary fruits must undergo drastic transformation from the original state, as we have seen in the story of New England. Human elements from an older society are torn out of their *milieu* and their complex of relationships in another land. They migrate as isolated families or individuals, for the most part. In their new home they gradually knit together to form new societies. How quickly they knit, and what kind of society they become depend on circumstances. On a hard frontier the values of the society are likely to be sternly utilitarian. The first concern is survival: the second is the accumulation of capital. These call for unceasing industry, frugality, cunning and ingenuity. Once the essentials have been secured and capital goods accumulated there *may* be (but there is no inevitability about it) a shift to such cultural, intellectual social and spiritual values as may feed the spirit, the imagination, the fancy, and the intellect, rather than the body.

The Art of Literature rests on the craft of letters, and is highly dependent on such things as language teachers, schools,

[1] Baker, Ray Palmer: *A History of English-Canadian Literature to the Confederation.* Cambridge and Toronto, 1920. P. 21.

colleges, libraries, clubs, printers, editors, publishers, critics and readers.   In its development it is likely to owe much to social intercourse and easy communication, and is thus assisted and accompanied by clubs, societies and other facilities for human interchange.   Behind any flowering of letters there is apt to be a swelling and upsurge and accumulation of such factors.   In the Nova Scotian story between the early settlements and the publication of *The Clockmaker* all these factors can be traced.

Perhaps it is not necessary to spell out the importance of these elements.   All of them were illustrated in the New England chapter.

One chief merit of schools and colleges is that they offer a meeting place of minds.   Through the miracle of the book, these contacts may transcend time and space.   In the classroom, the student associates with lively intellects in the flesh, but in the library he may be also instructed or quickened by words of Aristotle two millenia old, or of a living scholar resident far across the Atlantic but writing in the latest *Review*.

For the aspiring literary artist the college and the library offer the great service of familiarity with the best that older and far distant literary artists have accomplished.   Standards and models are available.

For the artist on the frontier such opportunities were likely to be few and meagre, and such as existed were therefore likely to be all the more precious.

It would be a rewarding study, I imagine, to trace the influence of the more important collections of books in pioneer British North America.

Through the vital link of the family cultural "cell," as discussed in an earlier chapter, it would be possible for children even in the heart of the isolated backwoods settlements to grow up aware of the possibilities of the literary art.

The influence of their parents and the small library carried with difficulty along primitive trails might be enough.

Even so, if an artist could be fostered and encouraged up to the point of early literary production, there would still remain, on the frontier, all the problems of reaching a public.

Outstanding manuscripts might well find printers and publishers in the great outside world. But native letters of any significance in British North America would obviously need to await the growth of the literary enterprises connected with the trade: printers, publishers, and booksellers.

The story of the press in British North America begins in Nova Scotia. A small hand-press set up by Bartholomew Green, Jr., at Halifax (taken there from Boston) is believed, Marie Tremaine reports, "to be the first to be used anywhere in the vast area now comprising Canada." Before Sam Slick there was considerable progress in this field in Nova Scotia, as will be illustrated.

A colony might wait a long time for a book-publishing industry. But in the meantime the early Gazettes and other Weeklies, and the first literary and religious magazines might provide a means whereby the aspiring frontier author could have the satisfaction of reaching a small audience. Examples of such fostering of beginning writers are frequently found in the story of Canadian literature.

Another useful study in the cultural story of Canada would be an account of its clubs and literary societies. Some references to these will be found woven into the narrative of later pages. It is interesting to note that Windsor, Nova Scotia, had a Reading Society as early as 1792.

With these general observations, let us return to the story of Nova Scotia letters.

There were four or five main waves of settlement into the Province. The first, concentrated principally at Halifax and along the South Shore, brought in 5,000 British and European soldiers and settlers. The Pre-Loyalists, chiefly native New Englanders and Britons Americanized by years of residence in the Thirteen Colonies, numbered another 8,000 or so, and occupied, among other areas, "the expropriated and vacant lands of the exiled Acadians." The Loyalists swelled the population of Nova Scotia by another 20,000. After the economic deflation in Europe which followed the Napoleonic Wars, there was another wave of migration, this time from the British Isles, notably from Scotland. The cumulative effect, as noted by Provincial Archivist D. C. Harvey, was that the population of Nova Scotia increased from less than 40,000 in 1784, to 80,000 in 1817, 120,000 in 1827 and 200,000 in 1837.[1]

For a time (1784-1789) it almost seemed as though a substantial body of educated immigrants moving *en masse* and over a relatively short distance, to country not unlike their homeland, might be able to continue their social and cultural life without any major disruption, carrying on in Nova Scotia almost where they had left off in New England. There must have been an impressive transfer of the apparatus of a literary and journalistic life. Baker says, for example, that the leading newspapers of Philadelphia were conveyed bodily to Nova Scotia. The migration of the Loyalists created virtually overnight in such centres as Shelburne, Halifax, and Windsor an appetite for education, for newspapers and for other literary productions. Shelburne for a time supported three newspapers!

Horton Academy opened in 1788, Halifax Academy in 1789, and King's College, Windsor (begun as an Academy in 1787) was incorporated in the same year. Also in 1789 there appeared the first issue of *The Nova Scotia Magazine*. It was printed by John Howe at Halifax and edited by William

[1]Harvey, D. C.: "The Intellectual Awakening of Nova Scotia," *Dalhousie Review*, April, 1933.

Cochran, a native of Ireland who had been professor of classics at King's College (now Columbia University) at New York. It was an ambitious venture containing eighty pages of double column text. Like the newspapers at Shelburne, this magazine was premature, and soon collapsed. Nor was it really a native venture, since editor and printer had come to the Province as mature men. The Nova Scotia community was not yet ready for a literary magazine: its circulation never quite attained the 300 mark, and after a year of struggle, Cochran left to join the teaching staff at King's College Windsor. Still, it survived for nearly three years, which was remarkable in a pioneer Province boasting a total population of 40,000. While it lasted, it offered a remarkable literary fare for a colony only a few years old.

After a brief period of stagnation following the collapse of the premature enterprises, more solid progress began. In his illuminating essay, *The Intellectual Awakening of Nova Scotia*, D. C. Harvey lists the main elements which may be taken as contributing to that awakening, culminating in the age of Haliburton and Howe. Various parts of the Province played their part. The Rev. Thomas McCulloch arrived at Pictou in 1803, became principal of the Pictou Grammar School in 1811, and in 1816 obtained an act of incorporation for Pictou Academy. Pictou became an intellectual and literary centre of sorts, *The Colonial Patriot* began publication there in 1827, and the Pictou *Observer* in 1831, the *Bee* in 1835. Among others, Joseph Howe paid tribute to the literary influence on him of "the Pictou Scribblers." Meantime, at Halifax, the *Acadian Recorder* had appeared in 1813 and the *Free Press* in 1816. An earlier paper, the *Weekly Chronicle*, reappeared as the *Acadian* in 1827. In 1824 the *Novascotian* or *Colonial Herald* came out, and in 1828 this paper was purchased by Joseph Howe, who, as Harvey says, "made of it the leading newspaper of British North America," so successful, indeed, that it "pushed off the market the two ambitious magazines that struggled for place and fame between 1826 and 1833—the *Acadian* and the *Halifax Monthly*."

Meantime, between 1811 and 1826, a series of educational statutes had provided for a grammar school in every county, and a common school in every community. In 1822, public subscription libraries were opened in Yarmouth and Pictou. Two years later the Halifax Public Library appeared, and in 1831 the Mechanics Library and Institute. In 1834 literary and scientific societies appeared in Pictou and Yarmouth; and in the same year the Halifax Athenaeum was founded. Seen against this cultural growth, the appearances of Nova Scotia's first literary works do not appear as isolated accidents. Rather they arrived in a society already in a state of intellectual ferment. Goldsmith was stirred to literary life by a Dramatic Society; Haliburton and Howe were active members of a literary Club which met at Howe's home to plan their papers for *The Novascotian*.[1]

Beneath these cultural manifestations, there was a solid economic and commercial foundation. "The fivefold increase in population from 1784 to 1837," wrote Alfred G. Bailey, "was accompanied by an accumulation of capital derived from a widening range of sources that included the increasingly effective utilization of natural products, skilled craftsmanship in the minor arts and in shipbuilding, and privateering and commerce on the high seas. The navigators returned enriched in experience from abroad, and the merchants, as Dr. Harvey has written, 'were forced by the nature of their vocations to examine provincial and international conditions' and were thus 'the first to break through traditional modes of thought, to arrive at intelligent conclusions.' "[2]

[1]Chittick, V. L. O.: *Thomas Chandler Haliburton, Sam Slick*. New York, 1924. P. 121; Longley, J. W.: *Joseph Howe*. Toronto, 1904. P. 9.
[2]*Dalhousie Review*, October, 1949. P. 237.

The three literary figures most prominent in the literary "Golden Age" of Nova Scotia are, of course, Oliver Goldsmith, Joseph Howe and Thomas Chandler Haliburton. The careers of each illustrate the conditions of frontier or pioneer letters. I shall not attempt either a biography or a criticism of their works, but a few interesting points in the life of each should be considered.

Oliver Goldsmith illustrates the suggestive power of a family tradition, as at a later date did the lives of Bliss Carman and Charles G. D. Roberts. Goldsmith's grandfather was the older brother of the eminent Irish-English playwright and novelist. The Canadian branch of the family was always conscious of the family link with the celebrity of the eighteenth century, and *The Rising Village*, the Canadian Goldsmith's only considerable literary work, was a sort of answer or North American sequel to the much more famous *The Deserted Village*.

The "Canadian" Oliver Goldsmith illustrates the Loyalist migration in one of its many variants. His father was a clergyman's son, born in Ireland, commissioned in the British Army, who served in the American Revolutionary War, married a Rhode Island girl, and at its close migrated to New Brunswick along with other Loyalist army officers. There, at St. Andrews, the "Canadian" Oliver Goldsmith was born in 1794. The family moved to Annapolis soon afterwards. By the time Oliver was a boy of six, the family was living at Halifax. As a lad, Oliver worked at a variety of tasks, none of them either very elevating or very profitable. Then he spent some time at the Halifax Grammar School, which was then under a graduate of Trinity College, Dublin. It is not possible to deduce from his autobiography that either of his teachers there struck any vital spark of letters within him: on the contrary, he dismisses his stay at the Halifax Grammar School as "worthless instruction," except for some progress he made in mathematics.

He then entered the Commissariat at Halifax and rose to be Deputy Assistant Commissary General.

His venture into the world of letters appears to have been fortuitous. It began when the Halifax Garrison, in 1822, established an "Amateur Theatre," and Oliver became a member of the cast. An opening address was solicited. Oliver wrote one: it was not accepted, but it was praised. Encouraged by the Anglican Bishop of Nova Scotia, Rt. Rev. John Inglis, and others, Goldsmith continued writing verse. Some time between 1822 and 1824 he wrote what his biographer calls "a pastoral poem of 528 lines" and it was published in 1825 in London by John Sharpe, a 48-page quarto offered for sale at half a crown.

There is some contemporary evidence that warm praise and encouragement greeted this first flight of a native-born Nova Scotian poet. However, there must have been scorn and criticism as well, since Oliver Goldsmith in his Autobiography, writing, I should think, long afterwards—perhaps as long as thirty years afterwards—reflected as follows:

I had better have left it alone. My unfortunate Baubling was torn to Shreds. My first effort was criticized with undue severity, abused, and condemned, and why? Because I did not produce a poem like the great Oliver. Alas! Who indeed could do so? Whatever merit it possessed in itself was disowned, because the genius that wrote it did not equal that of his great predecessor. I had, however, the approbation of the "judicious few" who thought it was an interesting Production. It was very fortunate for me that it was the occupation of leisure Hours. My living did not depend on my poetical talent, lucky fellow, and in this respect I had the advantage of the immortal poet. After this essay, I abandoned the Muses, and I have not had the pleasure of any further intercourse with the lovely ladies.[1]

---

[1] See the Autobiography, edited by W. E. Myatt, Toronto, 1943; also Biographical Society of Canada, Reprint Series No. 4. Toronto, 1950.

It throws a gleam of light on current conditions to add that the poem was sufficiently admired by a Montreal editor for him to quote it in its entirety in his review. Moreover, in 1834, while Goldsmith was stationed at Saint John, a second edition was produced there by John Macmillan. Other poems were included with it in "a small pocket volume in a neat silk binding, containing about 150 pages." It sold for five shillings.

The story of Joseph Howe illustrates another aspect of the Loyalist migration, this time with a much more substantial Yankee background. The Howes had crossed the Atlantic to Massachusetts in the seventeenth century. When the American Revolutionary War broke out, Joseph Howe's father was completing his apprenticeship as a printer in Boston. He attached himself to the British cause and at the end of the war migrated first to Newport and then to Halifax. He was a Tory in politics and a Sandemanian in religion. At Halifax he was appointed King's Printer and Postmaster General. Joseph Howe was born at Halifax in 1804. Despite the high-sounding titles of his father, the family income was modest and at thirteen Joseph began his own apprenticeship in the family printing office.

In the education of Joseph Howe the influence of his father and the ready access to classic works of literature were paramount. J. W. Longley, his biographer, says that Joseph was a voracious reader from boyhood on. His father was "a man of culture" who "devoted himself to the cultivation of the mind of his youngest son, who spent his winter evenings in reading and study . . ." His association with the Legislature, first as reporter and editor, later as politician and statesman, gave him access to one of the best collections of books in British North America. Longley quotes the legislative librarian at Halifax as declaring that Joseph Howe had read nearly all the books in the library.[1]

I find it significant that Haliburton, by far the most famous of the trio as a literary figure, was a beneficiary of several favourable factors unusual in frontier settlement. His grandfather, William Haliburton, migrated from Boston via Newport, to Piziquid (now Windsor) in the year 1763. Chittick says that Windsor was "already a settled district of respectable antiquity, having been early occupied by the Acadians, who were quick to see its advantages, and to discover the fertility of the surrounding river lands." Farming had begun there around 1680. The significant point about this is that the immigrant Pre-Loyalist villagers of Windsor were to a large extent spared several generations of absorption in the primary tasks of subduing the wilderness, which proved such a cultural setback to most of their cousins in the interior of British North America. In this village, already ancient by North American criteria, Thomas Chandler Haliburton was born in 1796. His mother died a year afterwards, and six years later his father married the daughter of one of the wealthiest and most prominent officials of Nova Scotia. As his father was an aggressive and successful business man, Haliburton had as a boy the advantages of wealth, and social connection not elsewhere common among second or third generation pioneers.

Windsor appears to have boasted a good classical Grammar School, which Haliburton attended, after which he went to King's College, founded in Windsor seven years before his birth. King's College suffered some limitations as a cradle of stimulating literary and intellectual life, since entry to it was then restricted by strictly applied ecclesiastical tests, but it had a famous library, founded on the gift of a Boston merchant, and one of the two learned doctors on the teaching staff was that same Rev. William Cochran who had edited the *Nova*

[1]Longley, *op. cit.* P. 3.

Scotia Magazine in 1789. Rev. Dr. Charles Porter, the president of King's, was a graduate of Oxford and a stimulating teacher; the courses were copied to some extent after those of Oxford and Cambridge, and it had the reputation of furnishing "admirable scholars" as well as "admirable gentlemen." Incidentally, Haliburton does not seem to have excelled as a student. Even if regional pride has somewhat magnified the reputation of this pioneer college, it is clear enough that Haliburton, in addition to advantages of family tradition, and a material ease, spent several years in residence in what was the most respectable academic atmosphere then available in British North America, under conditions far more favourable for one of the fine arts than most of his contemporaries could possibly find in other parts of the British subcontinent. D. C. Harvey praised the King's College of that period as contributing, through its library, its faculty and students, a great deal to the "intellectual awakening and diffusion of culture throughout the province."

Haliburton also enjoyed in his formative years the benefits of travel, of lively contact with older societies. Before he was twenty-one he had crossed the Atlantic twice, bringing back to Windsor on the second occasion an English wife. The next three years were busy in professional training for the bar, and when he was twenty-five or so he began the practice of law at Annapolis Royal. This was a small but interesting settlement, Tory in climate but with traditions of New England origin conducive to polite letters. (The principal of the High School at Annapolis was a Dartmouth man). Moreover Annapolis Royal was steeped in historical lore, as venerable as any site on the Peninsula. It was here that Haliburton began his active researches into the history and resources of Nova Scotia. His Provincial journeys brought him into contact with such valuable friends as the Loyalist Judge

Peleg Wiswall of Digby, a shrewd observer of the Provincial scene, with some instincts of the archivist.

As early as 1823, when Haliburton was twenty-seven, he had written and published a hand-book of information on the history and geography of Nova Scotia. In 1826, he ran as candidate for a county seat in the House of Assembly at Halifax and was elected. This provided an opportunity for him to gain from, and contribute to, the rising tide of intellectual and literary life of Halifax. He proved to be a witty and eloquent representative. In the Press Gallery, Joseph Howe was then covering the session for his weekly newspaper, *The Novascotian*. In February, 1827, Haliburton produced in the Assembly "a brilliant outburst of rhetoric," which so affected Joseph Howe, it is said, that "he forgot his note-taking and gave himself up wholly to the joy of listening." In as small a society as Halifax, it was almost inevitable that two such brilliant young men should be driven into one another's company. A long and intimate friendship developed which, however, was sorely tried for a time when Haliburton, in the Third Series of *The Clockmaker*, indulged in some transparent mockery of Joseph Howe as demagogue.[1]

It is not my aim here to try to document at any length this "creative moment" in the culture of the Maritime Provinces, but only to trace some of the evidences of cultural and social growth that culminated in the appearance of *The Clockmaker* in 1835. The years between Haliburton's arrival at Halifax and his first major work were years of intellectual and literary awakening. Not much of the literary activity of that period, it is true, has been able to survive the erosion of a century. Howe and Haliburton are still names to conjure with, but once you have dealt with them, there is not much left that rises above antiquarian interest or regional patriotism. The first literary work of any merit to be published in Nova Scotia was

[1]Chittick, *op. cit.* Chap. XV.

Haliburton's *History of Nova Scotia*, produced in 1829, as I have said, in the printing plant of Howe's *Novascotian*. It won Haliburton a government vote of thanks and an award of £500 but is said to have almost ruined the printer. It was a work of 800 pages and, except for inadequate proof reading (caused by Haliburton's father's illness), a credit to the printer and publisher.

Much of Haliburton's later work and the cream of Howe's literary production can still be read with great pleasure today. But the mountain peaks fall away to very modest foothills. Robert Christie, born and educated at Windsor, and thus in a sense a product of the period, was a dull historian but industrious chronicler. The names of Miss Tonge of Windsor, and Henry Clinch, a student of King's College, are still mentioned as verse writers of merit. Chittick, Haliburton's biographer, feels that the Halifax literary magazines printed work by native writers which "set in those early days a standard of sound literary taste that has not since been improved upon in Nova Scotian periodical publications." Nova Scotians tend to look back on that period as their golden age, but even a sympathetic historian like D. C. Harvey is driven to confess that "none of the poetry was very musical or very profound, while the controversial note in the prose writing, except in the odd historical or descriptive sketch, was very marked. By far the best literature was political with the exception of Howe's lectures on Eloquence and Shakespeare."

The measure of the Howe-Haliburton period is not, however, to be gauged solely on the merit of the actual literary works published. The influence of Howe was widespread and lasting. He "read and clipped intelligently from the Canadian, American, and British press, and so educated his fellow colonials in contemporary politics and letters." His political reviews stimulated active discussion. His descriptions of the scenery and resources of Nova Scotia spread among

Nova Scotians a knowledge of their own land.   He encouraged
the local poets and versifiers.   He made his paper a forum of
popular opinion.   He gathered around himself a group of
wits.[1]   Taking the career of Howe as a whole, it is a fair
inference that the future intellectual life of the Maritimes
owed him a great debt, and that the subsequent leavening
effect of Maritime character and learning on the rest of
Canada was in part a direct consequence of the Howe-
Haliburton flowering, in which Howe played so large a part.

[1]Chittick, *op. cit.*   P. 121.

CHAPTER VI

THE FRONTIER PROCESS IN UPPER CANADA

THE EARLY LITERARY STORY in what is now Ontario affords many useful illustrations of the frontier process at work. The cultural setback suffered by those immigrants who plunged into the heart of the continent was more severe than for the coastal Maritime settler. The severance from the homeland was more complete. Upper Canada exhibited no vigorous early flowering either of literature or other fine arts. The first hundred years of settlement was almost a blank so far as native *belles lettres* are concerned. At the date of the publication of Archibald Lampman's first book of lyrics (1888), it would not be far wrong to say that the only native Ontario writers of any enduring consequence had been Richardson and Charles Sangster. The bulk of what was called Canadian literature up to that date was the work of *émigrés* like Mrs. Moodie, Catherine Parr Traill, Alexander McLachlan, Isabella Valancy Crawford and William Kirby, writers who were not really the product of the Canadian environment in any significant way.

Nova Scotia, as we have seen, had been able to nurture a native literary blossoming in about three generations of settlement. One reason why no such intellectual and cultural quickening appeared in Upper Canada comes out in a comparison of the circumstances of the two settlements. Those favourable factors listed in the previous chapter were not present in Upper Canada. For one thing, the wholesale transporting of cultural apparatus into the hinterland was much more difficult. For another, the fragmentation of the societies was, on the whole, much greater. Mass or community migration into Upper Canada was not unknown, but on the whole I think that in the communities so transferred, a much smaller element of the literary and professional class went along. Apart from the Glengarry Highlanders and the Waterloo Mennonites, Upper Canada was settled essentially by scattered individuals and isolated families. As a generality, it cannot be maintained that the broad streams of migration between 1812 and 1841 included much very promising material for the early establishment of colleges, newspapers, libraries, magazines, printing houses, publishing houses, critical reviews or other prerequisites of a literary flowering. If the informants of Anna Brownell Jameson (in 1837) can be relied upon, in the more distant townships "not one person in twenty or thirty could read or write, or had the means of attaining such knowledge."[1]   Other skills were more to the point.   Most of the settlers in Upper Canada survived the tests of frontier life—they were industrious, frugal, spirited and stubborn; and in due course they and their descendants overcame all the physical obstacles of their rugged environment. But in the meantime, polite letters played only the smallest part in their activities or interests.

No one who has investigated the circumstances of the Ontario farm pioneers in the bush is likely to suppose that it

[1] *Winter Studies and Summer Rambles in Canada.*   Toronto, 1944.   P. 95.

could have been otherwise. The conditions of the North American frontier have been dwelt upon earlier. "The life of the pioneer was hard and stern," wrote R. J. Deachman, one-time federal member for Huron North, whose parents were pioneers in western Ontario. "He lacked modern equipment of the kind we now possess. With crude tools he cleared the land. It was a difficult task. If you doubt that statement, find a big green stump, fresh-cut, then try digging it out by the roots. Huge stones were removed by piling on top of them a load of old knots and limbs from the bush. They split the stones with fire, then carted them away. The work was arduous. It took the youth and spirit out of the pioneers. They were old at fifty."[1]

There was often in the first wave of settlement the thinnest margin between survival and starvation. There was a limit to the stores that could be taken into the bush, and in any event many pioneers lacked any financial margin: it was nip and tuck as to whether they could win through until the first substantial harvest. Settlers' effects were stripped to the barest essentials. Non-productive possessions were left behind, as were non-productive persons for the most part. In some primitive and nomadic communities elsewhere, living always on the edge of starvation, as among some tribes of Eskimos, the infirm and the aged have been ruthlessly rejected. On the frontier of Upper Canada no one would be turned out to starve, but everyone in the family was expected to pull his or her weight. There were slim pickings for the idler or the parasite, and an author might be classed as either, or both, judged by the pioneers' rugged values.

The greatest folly in pioneer days was to eat the seed corn. Yet immigrants were sometimes driven to it by starvation. Esther Clark Wright, in her account of the United Empire Loyalists of New Brunswick, narrates of certain early settlers

[1] In his *News Service No. 661*, written January 22, 1952.

on the present site of Fredericton that they had planted a few
potatoes in the spring of 1783, but when provisions failed to
arrive from the seaboard they were obliged to dig them up
again and eat them.   There is a similar reference in Peter Mc-
Arthur's *In Pastures Green.* "A late spring in the old days was a
real hardship," McArthur wrote, in one of his delightful rural
essays first published in the Toronto *Globe.*   "It meant more
than a delay in crops and spoiling the chances for a money-
making harvest.   The great question with the settlers during
the first few years was not money, but food.   A late spring
meant, time and again, that they were forced to eat their seed
grain and seed potatoes in order to preserve life.   I have just
read about one pioneer, and not one of the unthrifty kind,
either, who was forced to dig up the potatoes after they were
planted in order to feed his family."[1]

Virgin lands such as those of Upper Canada in the early
years of the nineteenth century attracted a great variety of
settlers.   These were "sorted out" through the formidable
screen of frontier life.   Samuel Thompson, a pioneer printer
of Toronto, left behind him an estimate of the sifting process
at work in the new lands north and west of Toronto in the
1820's and 1830's.   "Gentlemen" were almost always a
failure in such pioneer assaults.   With one or two exceptions,
Thompson writes, their investments and efforts resulted in
"absolutely nothing but wasted means and saddest memories."
Manual and skilled labourers were far more successful.   "If
we 'look upon this picture and on that'; if we compare the
results of the settlement of educated people and of the labouring
classes, the former withering away and leaving no sign
behind—the latter growing in numbers and advancing in
wealth and position until they fill the whole land, it is impossible to avoid the conclusion, that except as leaders and
teachers of their companions, gentlefolk of refined tastes and

[1] *In Pastures Green*, (Wells edn.).   Toronto, 1948.   Pp. 12-13.

of superior education, have no place in the bush, and should shun it as a wild delusion and a cruel snare."[1]

The pioneer records of Upper Canada throw lurid light on the values of the frontier and the difficulties of early authorship. The Stewart family, which located in 1823 north of the present site of Peterborough, the two Strickland sisters (Susanna Moodie and Catherine Parr Traill), who with their husbands pioneered in the Kawartha Lakes region in 1833-1834, and Anne Langton, who came out to the Bobcaygeon country in 1837, all wrote journals or preserved something of the times in letters to their relatives in the Old Country. From these, and from contemporary newspapers and magazines, the discouraging and even hostile conditions for the production of literary works in the backwoods country can be deduced. These accounts explain why no native literature could be expected for a long time from the frontier, and why even experienced and gifted writers, who came to the backwoods with their literary skills fully developed, and as inheritors of a long cultural tradition acquired in gentler surroundings, ceased for a while to produce anything more ambitious than family letters. They explain, too, why such cultured immigrants left behind them no immediate literary posterity, either among their own blood children or in the communities of native-born Canadians whom they met and influenced. The adverse influence of frontier life, in short, was capable not only of blocking the emergence of native artists, but also of killing off the literary ambitions of experienced writers among the immigrants.

During the first arduous years while Susanna Moodie was actually "roughing it in the bush" (northeast of the present city of Peterborough), she found it impossible to make any headway in her writing, though she had come to Canada at the

[1]Thompson, Samuel: *Reminiscences of a Canadian Pioneer*. Toronto, 1884, Chapter entitled "Society in the Backwoods."

age of twenty-nine as a published author, and had every incentive to continue, since she would have found even the most modest income from writing of incalculable benefit. Why her writing ceased is spelled out in dramatic detail in her best-known work. How she came to resume literary work will be recalled later.

Of all the arts, authorship asks least in the way of equipment. A pen, some ink, a few sheets of paper, and a few cents in postage would seem to cover the essentials. What we sometimes forget is that when the pioneer got far enough away from settled areas even these small essentials might be lacking or beyond his means. The use of red vegetable dye in lieu of ink (non-permanent, unfortunately), of birch bark as a substitute for paper, can be substantiated from pioneer records. Pine knots were sometimes used when candles were lacking.

We tend to forget, too, that postage was not always the nominal expense it is now, and that the mails of Upper Canada were primitive. "The post office, controlled from England, was even slower in its delivery than is suggested by the accounts of roads and travel," wrote D. D. Calvin of those days. "Mails arrived very irregularly in the settlements. Letters between Canada West and Britain were weeks on the way, and cost $1.12 via Canadian ports, but only 47 cents if sent, privately and illegally, via New York."[1] In 1820, charges were as high as 92 cents on a single letter from England to Quebec City. To the backwoods of Upper Canada the cost would be much higher. And it must be remembered that the dollar of those days represented several dollars in today's currency.

A makeshift lard-burner used by some frontier folk for lighting the cabin in the winter, a sort of Eskimo lamp, is an interesting illustration of F. J. Turner's remark that the

[1]Calvin, D. D.: *Queen's University at Kingston.* Kingston, 1944. P. 7.

wilderness drives the immigrant back to primitive devices. There was an additional discouragement to winter reading and writing in the cost of candles. No one would expect the pioneer to do much literary work in the busy summer season, but why could he not use the long winter nights for that purpose? As James Truslow Adams has shown, even this was not so simple as it sounds. "Common sale candles" in 1761 cost one and three-quarter pence per hour of illumination. Adams calculates that in U.S. currency of 1927 this amounted to $8 a month for the light of a single candle.[1] (In 1957 money, the cost would be $15 a month.) Such sums, he says, would obviously be prohibitive for most households. Research into Upper Canada costs would probably show similar figures. The invention of the Franklin stove and the introduction of coal oil lamps greatly increased the convenience of frontier homes, and made it more likely that some reading and writing could be done in the long winter evenings, but the earliest log cabins were bare of any such luxuries.

In addition to the passive handicaps of frontier conditions, some writers had to face active hostility to the practice of literature, if one can rely on Mrs. Moodie's observations. She implies that the frontier was not only non-literary but could be aggressively anti-literary. "The sin of authorship meets with little toleration in a new country," she wrote. The Moodies, she said, were reckoned no addition to the society of the Ontario town where they lived for a time. "Authors and literary people they held in supreme detestation."

Mrs. Moodie was told by a lady, the very first time she appeared in company, that "she heard that I wrote books, but she could tell me that they did not want a Mrs. Trollope in Canada." Another of her self-constituted advisers, she writes, informed her, with great asperity in her look and tone, that it

[1]Adams, James Truslow: *Provincial Society*. P. 303.

would be better for her to lay by the pen, and betake herself
to some more useful employment; that she (Mrs. Moodie's
adviser) thanked her God that she could make a shirt, and
see to the cleaning of her house.

"Anxious not to offend them," the author adds, "I tried
to avoid all literary subjects." She was accustomed, she says,
to hear the whispered remark, or to have it retailed to her by
others, "oh, yes, she can write, but she can do nothing else."[1]

It is, of course, possible that Mrs. Moodie misinterpreted
some of these incidents. At the root of the hostility of the
pioneer native North American women may have been a
natural resentment at Mrs. Moodie's assumption of social
superiority. The pioneer women may have secretly envied
her talent and experience; and their derogatory remarks about
such idle accomplishments as authorship may not have
stemmed from active animosity toward writing as such. But
the salvation of the pioneer lay, as has been stressed, in other
more practical and non-literary achievements. On the
frontier, the dilettante, the bookworm, the rhymester, the
dreamy philosopher might rank alike as parasites or idlers,
non-producers of the essentials without which the frontier
was doomed.

Another frontier enemy of literary activity was the absence
of social and cultural stimulation. This comes out in many
accounts. Even those who had plunged into the frontier
carrying in their heads a good store of accumulated literary
and philosophical lore soon found themselves becoming stale
and out-of-touch. Even when they migrated in a body from
more advanced cultural areas this held true. The trek of the
United Empire Loyalists to Nova Scotia and New Brunswick
has been looked at. It will be recalled that among the
U.E.L. refugees to Nova Scotia, there were many clergymen,

[1]*Our Sense of Identity*, edited by Malcolm Ross. Toronto, 1954,
Pp. 10-11.

barristers, judges and civil and military officials, graduates of Harvard and other institutions. They contributed considerably to the literary activity of the Maritimes. But even such wholesale transfusions of culture generally underwent rapid decay. Ray Palmer Baker notes that ". . . their activities must have been seriously curtailed by their emigration. Their letters, always in good taste, reflect the narrowness of pioneer life. The writers had little time for anything beyond the daily routine essential to existence. Surveying, the construction of wagon roads, and the clearing of farms do not tend toward *belles lettres*. Though the Loyalists left many intimate records of their labours and diversions, they are too uniformly practical to be of interest."

The story of the Upper Canada immigrants illustrates the process at work. Anne Langton, for example, emigrated with her family to the Sturgeon Lake region (near the present town of Fenelon Falls) in 1837. Anne was thirty-three, and had travelled widely on the continent of Europe; she had studied art in Rome and was an accomplished musician. (Her brother John later became Auditor-General for the Government of Canada and Vice-Chancellor of the University of Toronto.) The Langtons came out from the Manchester-Liverpool region of England; and they settled in the region north of Peterborough at the same time as a number of other well-to-do and well-educated English families. H. H. Langton (who edited the *Journals*) says that a great part of the shore of Sturgeon Lake was occupied by English "gentlemen," some of them University men; he quotes John Langton in a letter of August, 1833, as follows: "On Sturgeon Lake you will find six settlers. Certainly this is not many, but then four of them have been at a University, one at the Military College at Woolwich, and the sixth, though boasting no such honours, has half a dozen silver spoons and a wife who plays the guitar." Another settlement a few miles to the east contained the Stewarts, and, as distant neighbours of the Stewarts, the Stricklands, Moodies, and Traills.   In a sense these settlements in what was called the "Newcastle District" of Upper Canada formed a parallel to the U.E.L. settlements in the Maritimes, in that there were clusters of university people and bookish and cultured families, to leaven the North American native stock of skilful pioneers and toughened frontier craftsmen.   But Anne Langton's *Journals* show the same deadening influence of the "back country": the flame of transplanted "bookishness" and urbane culture fading under the engrossing exactions and ruthless demands of pioneer struggle.   After two years on the fringe of settlement, Anne reports, under date of July 2, 1839:

We have had a thunderstorm today.   My mother amused herself during the storm with repeating poetry, a thing I have not done for a very long time.   The old world is the world of romance and poetry.   I daresay our lakes, waterfalls, rapids, canoes, forests, Indian encampments, sound very well to you dwellers in the suburbs of a manufacturing town; nevertheless I assure you there cannot well be a more unpoetical and anti-romantic existence than ours.

Nine months earlier, in October, 1838, Anne Langton had put her finger on one of the deadening and dampening effects of the frontier:

The greatest danger, I think, we all run from our peculiar mode of life is that of becoming selfish and narrow-minded. We live so much to ourselves and mix so exclusively with one community.   It is not only that the individuals are few, but the degrees and classes we come in contact with are still more limited.   Those who have come to this country before their thinking and feeling years ought, I think, all to go back to the old world for a time, just to look above and below them; and how many more new emotions they would have to experience!   Here we know that the world is wide, but we do

not feel its wideness. . . . We certainly do not gain many
new ideas, and must consequently fall a little behind our age.[1]

Reference has been made to the Stewart family, Frances
and Thomas. Frances Stewart was born in England in 1794,
and was a relation of Maria Edgeworth, or so it was said.
She emigrated to Canada in 1822. In her letters home, Mrs.
Stewart reflected the feelings of the educated and cultured
immigrants. Canadian backwoods life was insupportable to
those who had lived in a round of amusements or had enjoyed
intellectual or scientific society, she thought. The Stewarts
possessed a library of some importance in such a non-literary
land. Among those who owed a debt to it was Catherine
Parr Traill. The Stewarts tried hard, it would seem, to
maintain in the Peterborough backwoods some of the cultural
life of the Mother Country. Members of the family would
read aloud while others worked. But even so, Mrs. Stewart
complained that the young people, including her own ten
children, showed a want of ideas and conversation, a dearth
of intellectual pursuits and too much confinement to the
business of the day. It seems to be characteristic that
the literary and scholarly fire of the first generation which
migrates from centres of culture soon dies down.

Esther Clark Wright, in the work already cited, illustrates
this process at work in New Brunswick. The main body of
settlers had arrived in the 1780's. "The decade of the
1820's," she writes, "was a transition period, when the
process of handing on to the next generation was completed
by the Loyalists of 1783. The few old men and old women,
who remembered another, more civilized *milieu*, reminisced
unheeded. The sons of the Loyalists knew only the frontier
life, two-thirds lumbering, one-third farming; their formal
education had been neglected and they could barely read or

[1] *A Gentlewoman in Upper Canada.* Toronto, 1950. P. 73.

write; the land they inherited was sufficiently cleared for the
subsistence type of farming which was all they knew; it was no
longer a brave new world, and apathy succeeded the deter-
mination of the previous generation."[1] And of Upper
Canada, another historian quoted F. J. Turner: "Thus does
culture sag, once the old originals who brought something
with them from a larger world are gone, and the natives are
left in their own intellectual desert."[2]

The fading of the flame, the wilting of the culture, can be
seen at work in many accounts of pioneer life. The historians
of New England noted it: ". . . in the writings of the men
who settled Massachusetts or visited it in the earliest period,
there is a freshness and charm of outlook and phrase which
allures the reader even of today. In Smith or Bradford,
Higginson or Wood, one feels in the presence of a healthy
mind, actively interested in this world or the next; but, when
these men have passed, the balance of the century leaves us
hardly a work which, for a modern reader, possesses any
interest other than antiquarian or historical."[3]

Sir J. G. Bourinot, in his examination of Canada's intellectual development, recalls, in this connection, the deadly
effects of isolation on the frontier, "making even the better class
narrow-minded, selfish, and at last careless of anything like
refinement." This stagnation was broken only at rare
intervals "through the visit of some intelligent clergyman
or tourist." No considerations of pioneer life, he adds, should
ignore the visits of these products of a more cultured society.
Writing of the 1830's, Bourinot says: "Then, as always in
Canada, there were found among the clergy of all denomina-
tions hardworking, self-denying priests and missionaries who

[1]*Op. cit.*, pp. 229-230.
[2]A. R. M. Lower, in *Canadian Journal of Economics and Political Science*,
February, 1942.
[3]Adams, James Truslow: *The Founding of New England*. Boston, 1927.
Pp. 370-371.

brought from time to time to some remote settlement of the provinces spiritual consolation, and to many a household, long deprived of the intellectual nourishment of other days, an opportunity of conversing on subjects which in the stern daily routine of their lives in a new country were seldom or ever talked of."[1]

Perhaps here and there it was not so much that the literary flame died out as that the intellectual and imaginative faculties were diverted into other channels, in the process of challenging the physical obstacles and of mastering the frontier environment. James Truslow Adams, discussing intellectual life in the American colonies a hundred years after the first seacoast settlements, wrote:

> The university-bred and other cultured men who had come from England and elsewhere had not realized the magnitude and absorptive power of the task of subduing the forest. By degrees they had found their energies diverted into new and more material channels. Many a one must have echoed Pastorius when even he said, in a moment of discouragement in his Philadelphia outpost in the wilderness, that "never have metaphysics and Aristotlian logic earned a loaf of bread." Not only the work to be done but the rewards to be gained must have led many, as we have already noted in speaking of the clergy, to abandon the life of the spirit for that of active business.[2]

Quite enough has been said about the hostile environment for native letters on such frontiers as Upper Canada in the early years of the nineteenth century. It is time now to turn to some of the first manifestations of native and *émigré* letters in that part of British North America. Some of these modest achievements serve to underline the handicaps.

Upper Canada as late as 1783 is described by one of our

[1]Bourinot, J. G.: *Canada's Intellectual Strength and Weakness.* Royal Society of Canada's series No. 1, published 1893, p. 10.
[2]Adams, James Truslow: *Provincial Society.* P. 114.

leading historians as "empty save for a few Indians." However, by 1812 the population had risen to seventy or eighty thousand, nearly all conveniently located along the River and Lake "Front" from Montreal to Windsor. But the first booklet of verse was not printed in Upper Canada until 1822. The first book of any significance published in Upper Canada appears to have been a history of the War of 1812. It was printed at Niagara in 1832; and the fate of the author was characteristic and symbolic. The venture failed, and the author spent a term in prison as a result of his inability to settle the printer's account.

Since the frontier was so hostile, how does one explain the figure of John Richardson, whose literary works began to appear as early as the 1820's? His boyhood was spent in pioneer communities singularly lacking in the accepted stimuli of literary creation: schools, colleges, libraries, printing plants and the like. Yet in some ways he was as ambitious an author as Canada, has ever seen. His published works of prose and verse number fifteen or more, and he had the audacity to want to be a professional fulltime author.

The larger community in which Richardson lived was certainly barren soil for the literary artist, as his career later proved. The explanation for his emergence at all must come from his family inheritance and environment. John Richardson's father, of Jacobite stock, was an officer in Simcoe's Queen's Rangers, a surgeon who later became Judge of the Western District of Upper Canada. His mother was of Jacobite descent, too, on her father's side; his maternal grandmother was the daughter of an aristocratic French family. This French strain explains why the novelist's mother had received her education at La Congregation de Notre Dame, then described as "the chief educational institution of Lower Canada." The inference was very strong that John Richardson, though raised on the edge of the wilderness, benefited

from a home environment quite unusual in its refinement and
literary culture: it was, moreover, a bilingual home, and John
Richardson became as fluent in French as in English.

His ablest work, the novel *Wacousta*, had a fair reception in
the United States, but his own people, the Canadians,
ignored it. "Not more than one twentieth were aware of the
existence of the book," he wrote, "and of that twentieth, not
one-third cared a straw whether the author was a Canadian
or a Turk." A sequel to *Wacousta* entitled *The Canadian
Brothers* or *The Prophecy Fulfilled*, was brought out in an
edition of 250 in the year 1840. "I published in Canada,"
Richardson wrote of the venture afterwards. "I might as well
have done so in Kamschatka." Unable to make a living from
his writing in Canada, Richardson finally turned to New York.
Even there he appears to have starved to death, after selling
his faithful dog so as to buy food![1]

Susanna Moodie's Canadian writing was contemporaneous
with that of Richardson, but the circumstances of its appearance were of another sort. Mrs. Moodie came of a literary
family of Suffolk, England, and was already a confirmed
writer when she and her husband arrived in Upper Canada.
They plunged into the bush, for which they were not prepared
by training or background, and in the hard life which followed
her literary ambitions were smothered. That she became an
author once more was a tribute to the long-range stimulation
of a literary event in the city of Montreal, over two hundred
miles away. A literary Irishman named John Lovell had
come to Canada in 1820, a man destined to play a distinguished role in early Canadian publishing. In 1837 he was
chiefly instrumental in the founding of the magazine *The
Literary Garland* at Montreal. This was, as it proved, the
spark which was to re-ignite Mrs. Moodie's creative ambitions.
Her account of its role in her life has become a familiar story:

[1]Riddell, W. R.: *John Richardson*. Toronto, 1923. P. 21.

In the winter of 1837-1838 John Lovell wrote to her asking
her to contribute articles, stories and poems, and promising
remuneration for her labours.   Mrs. Moodie wrote later:

Such an application was like a gleam of light springing up
in the darkness; it seemed to promise the dawning of a brighter
day.   I had never been able to turn my thoughts toward
literature during my sojourn in the bush.   When the body is
fatigued with labour, unwonted and beyond its strength, the
mind is in no condition for mental occupation.

The year before, I had been requested by an American
author, of great merit, to contribute to the *North American
Review*, published for several years in Philadelphia; and he
promised to remunerate me in proportion to the success of the
work.   I had contrived to write several articles after the
children were asleep, though the expense even of the stationery
and the postage of the manuscripts was severely felt by one so
destitute of means; but the hope of being the least service to
those dear to me cheered me to the task.

I never realized anything from that source, but I believe it
was not the fault of the editor.   Several other American
editors had written to me to furnish them with articles, but I
was unable to pay the postage of heavy packets to the States,
and they could not reach their destination without being
paid to the frontier.   Thus, all chance of making anything in
that way had been abandoned.

I wrote to Mr. L—— and frankly informed him how I was
situated.   In the most liberal manner, he offered to pay the
postage of all my manuscripts to his office, and left me to name
my own terms of remuneration.

This opened up a new era in my existence, and for many
years I have found this generous man, to whom I am still
personally unknown, a steady friend.   I actually shed tears of
joy over the first twenty-dollar bill I received from Montreal.
It was my own; I had earned it with my own hand; and it
seemed to my delighted fancy to form the nucleus out of which
a future independence for my family might arise.

I no longer retired to bed when the labours of the day were
over.   I sat up and wrote by the light of a strange sort of
candle that Jenny called "sluts," and which the old woman

manufactured out of pieces of old rags twisted together and dipped in pork lard, and stuck in a bottle.   They did not give a bad light, but it took a great many of them to last me for a few hours.

The faithful old creature regarded my writings with a jealous eye.

"An', shure, it's killing yerself that you are intirely.   You were thin enough before you took to the pen; scriblin' and scrablin' when you should be in bed an' asleep.   What good will it be to your childher, dear heart! if you die afore your time, by wastin' your strength afther that fashion?"

Jenny never could conceive the use of books.   "Shure we can live and die without them.   It's only a waste of time botherin' your brains wid the like of them; but, thank goodness! the lard will soon all be done, an' thin we shall hear you spakin' again, instead of sittin' there doubled up all night, destroying your eyes wid porin' over the dirthy writin'."[1]

John Lovell's new magazine was edited by a relative, John Gibson, aided by a Mrs. Frederick Cushing.   The intentions of the magazine are set forth in Vol. 1, No. 3, as that of "gathering the gems of Canadian literature and enshrining them into the pages of *The Garland*."   The figure of speech may have been a trifle inflated, but the design was beyond reproach.   The critical reader who works his way through those pages today may cringe a bit at some of the "gems" the editor gathered, but the overall impression is one of a worthy and influential pioneer enterprise.

The first issue, dated December, 1838, drew freely from standard British authors (for example, an extract was printed from Lockhart's *Life of Scott*), but the intention to stress Canadian subjects was shown by a poem on The Saint Lawrence, a "rhapsody" on Lake St. Charles, and an elegy on The Death of Montcalm.   Early issues relied upon Charles Dickens, Harry Lever and Robert Montgomery (the minor

[1]Moodie, Susanna: *Roughing It in the Bush*.   Toronto, 1923.   Pp. 425-427.

poet of Bath, who wrote visions of death and hell, and a poem about Satan which drew down upon his head the denunciation of Macaulay), but the Canadian content of the magazine steadily grew.

Susanna Moodie first appears in the May, 1839, issue, with a poem on The Otonobee, and "a loyal song for Canada" entitled "The Oath of the Canadian Volunteers" (This is an echo of the Mackenzie Rebellion of 1837). Mrs. Moodie begins a novel on the instalment plan shortly afterwards. It is entitled *The Royal Quixote*. Mrs. Anna B. Jameson is represented by a poem on Niagara Falls. The author of *Wacousta*, John Richardson, appears with certain chapters of a sequel to that tale, *The Two Brothers*. (It was the interest shown by readers of *The Literary Garland* in these instalments in magazine form, according to the author, that led to the publication of *The Two Brothers* in book form in the following year, to which reference has been made earlier.)

Montreal in 1840 was the commercial capital of the lower St. Lawrence, with a population (partly French-speaking) of about 35,000. Its economic future was bright. But the potential readership for a literary magazine in English was still very limited, and it is not surprising to read, within a year of the first issue, an appeal by the editor for "some assistance in pecuniary matters" from his friends. This appeal seems to have been adequately answered. In a subsequent issue he gives thanks to contributors, the press, and the people. "Their united favours have solved the problem, whether a literary plant may exist and flourish."

Having survived this first financial crisis, *The Literary Garland* went on to publish another novel, *The Fugitive*, by Mrs. Moodie, which the editor greeted with the proud announcement that "this spirited tale" was included in a number "which is almost entirely composed of original contributions." From this it would appear that the existence of a native magazine had stimulated native and immigrant writers to new heights of activity. In July, 1840, the editor is exultant over the literary quickening. "It would not have been believed," he writes, "some two years since, that a monthly the size of this magazine would be too small to contain all the *accepted* originals which would be voluntarily furnished to it."

Some of Charles Sangster's verse appeared in *The Literary Garland* years before any of it was gathered in book form. The first novel by Rosanna Eleanor Mullins (later Mrs. Leprohon) appeared in serial form. Catherine Parr Traill was among the contributors. *The Literary Garland* stayed alive for thirteen years, and though it is impossible to measure its creative stimulus in any statistical way, it was obviously considerable.

In a chapter meant to illustrate the fate of early native letters in Upper Canada it would be out of place to do more than mention in passing the Scottish immigrant poet Alexander McLachlan or the dramatist Charles Heavysege, since neither of them was born or reared in Canada. In addition, Heavysege lived in what is now the Province of Quebec. But an incident or two from their experience serves to throw further light on the state of authorship at the time, whether native or *émigré*. McLachlan was certainly as popular a poet as was to be found in English-speaking Canada just before Confederation, and was ranked by one critic of discernment with Sangster, yet to publish his best book of poems he laid out a sum which involved him in financial embarrassment for years to come. Charles Heavysege even won some international reputation with the publication of the drama *Saul*, and a student is impressed to learn that the work ran into three Canadian editions. What is not so comforting is that the second edition appeared only because a fellow-member of the Montreal Literary Club (who, it is reported, could ill afford it) put up the cost of printing it, and that when Charles Heavysege died in 1876 the bill for the third edition remained unpaid. So much for the most distinguished of the mid-century poets!

Charles Sangster (1822-1893) stands out as the first native-born poet to win much reputation in the Province of Canada. His life illustrates once more the rude fate of the aspiring artist in a hard utilitarian setting. He was born at Kingston, the son of a joiner in the British Navy. His father died when he was only two, and his mother was left with a large family to raise. Charles went to work at fifteen; if we can take him at his word his limited schooling was virtually worthless. His literary efforts had to be squeezed out of a life of constant toil and economic insecurity. Books and the newspaper press of Upper Canada provided a limited stimulus and outlet for his writings. He took for his poetic models the work of such English poets as Collins, Gray, and Byron; and it can be argued that his poetry was already old-fashioned long before he published it. Such a time-lag is characteristic of colonial poets. His first volume (1856) was printed by public sub-scription, which in blunt language means that Sangster neither possessed the funds to print it himself nor could find a publisher prepared to underwrite the cost. John Lovell of Montreal and John Creighton of Kingston brought out his second volume in 1860, but apparently at the author's expense. When he was forty-six, he accepted a position in the Post Office Department at Ottawa. No further work came from his pen. W. D. Lighthall, writing while Sangster was still alive, asserted that his nervous system "was broken down by the grind of newspaper toil and civil service tread-milling" and J. W. Garvin later surmised that "his poetic energy and ambition succumbed to the incessant drudgery and to the hampering cares of ill-paid employment." There is ample evidence that at least a few of his fellow Canadians thought highly of his work, but it is clear that neither his reception nor the sale of his works was such as to induce him to go on producing or publishing after the age of thirty-eight.

How little financial inducement there was for even a sort of poet laureate to persist in his labours in those days appears in an anecdote related by John Reade. John Lovell of Montreal carried on his books an unpaid balance which Sangster owed for the printing of *Hesperus and Other Poems*. Years passed, and Lovell had forgotten the debt. But one day he received a remittance in full. Sangster explained that he had obtained a position at Ottawa in the Post Office. "In this accession of good fortune," writes Reade, "Sangster had at once thought of his printer in Montreal."[1]

The state of polite letters in the Province of Canada three years before Confederation is well described in Canada's first comprehensive anthology of poetry. Edward Hartley Dewart compiled, and John Lovell of Montreal printed, *Selections from Canadian Poets*, "with occasional Critical and Biographical Notes, and an Introductory Essay on Canadian Poetry." The Rev. E. H. Dewart, who like Lovell was of Irish birth, had come to the county of Peterborough with his parents at the age of six. He became in due course editor of *The Christian Guardian*, and one of Canada's first literary essayists. In the 1864 anthology, he deplored the neglect of native letters in Canada. He listed, besides the handicap of pioneer pre-occupation with bare necessities, and the scarcity of wealth and leisure, the prevalence of low and false conceptions of poetry, the colonial position of Canada, the competition of English books and magazines, and the sentimental attachment of recent immigrants to the literature of the Mother Country. Native poets, he said, were met with contempt in some quarters, and elsewhere greeted with indiscriminate praise that tended to mislead the public and

[1]*Canada, An Encyclopaedia*, Vol. V, p. 155.

give the authors themselves false notions of their talents and achievements. Canadian booksellers, he said, favoured the sale of British and American works on which they made larger profits and looked askance at native productions. If Canadian poetry was crude and imperfect, the cause was largely to be found in the want of educational advantages. Dewart thought it was a wonder under the circumstances that so much good work had been produced. "Some of our most gifted poets," he wrote, "after ineffectual efforts to gain the attention and approval of the public, have despairingly turned to more hopeful, though less congenial labours, feeling that their choicest strains fell on listless ears, and unsympathetic hearts."[1] This might almost be considered standard comment for any colony in the pioneer stages.

[1]*Selections from Canadian Poets.* P. xvii.

CHAPTER VII

PIONEER AUTHORS IN FRENCH-SPEAKING CANADA

THE CANADIAN student who wishes to read in English some account of the beginnings of literature in French-speaking Canada will seek far and find little. Ray Palmer Baker's excellent history is expressly confined to English-Canadian literature. The works of Messrs. Logan and French, V. B. Rhodenizer, Dr. Lorne Pierce, and Sir Charles G. D. Roberts include short studies. Archibald MacMechan wrote a charming chapter in *Headwaters of Canadian Literature*. Mason Wade's *The French Canadians* contains much fascinating detail, especially on literary activity in the mid-nineteenth century. But a definitive work in English remains to be written.

The following sketch is no more than an attempt to illustrate the "frontier thesis" by a few notes on the early letters of French-speaking Canada.

New France was settled by similar ethnic stock to that of New England, in the sense that both were products of the Western European cultural tradition. The environment of the new home was not essentially different. But the differences were substantial, if one looks below the surface. The kind of society from which each came, and the philosophy and politics of settlement, were miles apart. The contacts of Quebec with the mother country were more intermittent, and for a while were broken off almost completely. Much of Quebec was located on tidewater, and Montreal on a great river, but communications with Europe were severed by ice for several months of the year, even when other barriers were absent. The story of early French-language letters is, naturally, quite different from that of New England or even of Nova Scotia. Yet in a number of interesting ways, the story reflects all the circumstances of colonial writing noted in earlier chapters.

For one thing, all the early literary productions of New France were the work of discoverers, explorers, founders, and visitors. A native literature was extremely slow in appearing. When it did finally emerge, it was subject to all the hardships and discouragements noticed in the story of Upper Canada.

Thus the story of letters in New France begins with such names as Cartier, Marc Lescarbot and Champlain. Jacques Cartier wrote the story of his voyages. Lescarbot, the literary lawyer, celebrated Port Royal in verse and prose. Champlain wrote of his adventures as an explorer. Récollets and Jesuits left behind them vivid accounts of their missionary expeditions among the Indians. These form a part of the literature of Quebec in the same sense as Captain John Smith's *History of Virginia*, or the *Journal* of William Bradford and Edward Winslow form a part of American literature. But they are far from being native letters in any sense. Marc Lescarbot, for example, was thirty-six when he sailed with Champlain; his *History of New France* was printed, published and distributed in Paris.

Many such names dot the early pages of our literary chronicles in both languages. They preserved valuable impressions of the new land and its pioneer society, but their books have little or no relevance in any examination of native letters. Indeed, if we set aside, in the story of French-Canadian letters up to 1760, all the persons born elsewhere, all the persons who came to New France intellectually mature, we are left only with such obscure figures as Nicholas Jérémie or Sister Saint-Ignace.

One looks in vain for any native literary flowering among the early generations of French-speaking settlers born along the St. Lawrence River. Explanations for this silence can be readily supplied, but it is perhaps sufficient here to recall that there is no evidence that a printing press ever operated in New France or Acadia before the fall of Quebec in 1759. Is a native literature remotely possible without even a single printer, a single publisher or a single bookstore in the community?

The time-lag between first settlement and the appearance of a native literature was greater, indeed, in the French-speaking colonies of North America than anywhere else. If Garneau and Ferland are to be taken as the first significant figures in French-Canadian letters (as Octave Crémazie seems to have regarded them), then a gap of almost 250 years yawns between the founding of Quebec and the emergence of the first native French-language literature of national importance. Why did Quebec remain so long without a literature of her own? The most illuminating answer I have run across is supplied by J. B. Brebner in his *North Atlantic Triangle*:

Although the British and French colonists were basically not very different as political beings, they were far apart in culture. The British Americans were the heirs of a thorough going Protestant Reformation and of the unquestioned secular fame of Newton and Locke. They lived in an atmosphere of free inquiry which was continuously freshened by the printed works which crossed the Atlantic, hot from the press, to be noted in colonial newspapers and discussed by many inquisitive minds. In addition, North America was an almost perfect environment for the acquisitive Puritan ethic which had rooted itself firmly in seventeenth century England.

But the intellectual spirit of the settlements in New France was radically different, as Brebner makes clear:

The French, on the other hand, were children of, and actors in, the Catholic Counter-Revolution. Their very colony was almost as much a product of the missionary spirit of the seventeenth century as it was of commercial or political enterprise. Their core of culture was the Catholic classicism upon whose broad foundation the more worldly cultivation of Louis XIV's Court at Versailles had been raised. The corrosive ideas of the eighteenth century philosophers which were steadily undermining the *ancien regime* in France, had reached only a few private libraries in New France, and had been kept from the populace because the colony had no printing press and the Church saw to it that, except for a few technical accomplishments for boys and girls, education should be almost exclusively *ad majorem Dei gloriam*. What scepticism and worldliness there were amounted to little more than the natural individualism of self-reliant, if slightly cultivated men.[1]

If the term literature is to be narrowly confined to *printed* material, then perhaps the history of New France is made to appear exceptionally barren. It is necessary to remember that the colonists of New France treasured and handed on to their children a great store of folk poetry, folk songs and folk tales, which, no doubt, served the same social and spiritual ends as does printed matter in a more bookish society. There is a certain unreal snobbishness about our exclusive emphasis on the printed word. But so far as a native printed literature is concerned, the conditions in Quebec were quite unfavourable until after the fall of New France. After that, in the next three or four generations, all of the essential prerequisites leading up to a native printed literature made their appearance: dynamic changes in the

[1]Brebner, J. B.: *North Atlantic Triangle*. Toronto, 1945. P. 34.

society itself, the importation of printing presses, the inaugura-
tion of newspapers and magazines, the emergence of printers,
editors and publishers, the opening of book stores, the establishment of libraries, and a stimulating renewal of intellectual
contact with the mother country, France.

The fortunes of war and a sense of political subservience, a
resentment of it, indeed, turned the thoughts of the French-
speaking North Americans back to their illustrious past: there
began to appear archivists, antiquarians and historians; and
at the same time a small but receptive reading public came
into being, prepared to encourage their activities. The birth
of French-language letters in Canada was slow and painful,
and the treatment of pioneer authors as callous and unimagina-
tive as usual. Nevertheless, here as elsewhere in North
America, a native literature of great community value and
creditable technical skill did eventually come into being.

The weekly newspaper and the magazine played at least as
important a role in the development of the French-language
authors of Quebec in the nineteenth century as in English-
speaking Canada. Michel Bibaud's pedestrian verse appeared
in *L'Aurore*, Garneau's early historical writing in Etienne
Parent's *Le Canadienne*, and in his own *L'Abeille Canadienne* and
L'Institut. Bibaud's *La Bibliotheque Canadienne* provided a
medium for a number of Quebec authors. A group of writers
launched *Les Soirées Canadiennes* in 1861: in it appeared
Gérin-Lajoie's novel, *Jean Rivard*, and the popular tales of
LaRue and Taché. *Le Foyer Canadien* fostered the work of
established French-Canadian writers. These are only a few
of the publications which offered the literary figures of Quebec
a means of finding expression in the years before book
publishing was a well-established industry.

Comparative dates are of little significance, but it is interesting that the first peaks of literary achievement in French
appear around 1860, that is, about midway between the

climax of the Halifax-Windsor school and the emergence of the Fredericton Group, of Carman, Roberts and Sherman. The "foothills and climbing lesser ranges"—to repeat Pratt's fine imagery, were represented in French-speaking Canada by such men as Bibaud and Parent, by Jacquer Viger, and Georges-Barthelemi Faribault, antiquarians and archivists, who at least preserved and collected literary material for the later edification and inspiration of more creative minds.

Mason Wade agrees with earlier writers in singling out François-Xavier Garneau as the real father of French-Canadian literature. Tradition reports that Garneau was nettled into a lifelong arduous dedication to the immortalizing of Quebec's glorious past, as professional historian, by the taunt of an English-speaking fellow clerk. Garneau is said to have replied: "I shall write the history which you do not even know exists." He prepared himself for his task by steeping himself in the literary and scientific classics in a library owned by the Quebec lawyer to whom he was articled. This was followed by visits to Europe and by two years' residence in London. Before his first book appeared, Garneau had contributed extensively to Etienne Parent's newspaper, and to short-lived periodicals which he himself had founded. His study of Jacques Cartier (1842) was followed in 1845 by the first volume of his history of Canada, the second volume appearing in 1846, and the third in 1848. These works won him honours at home and a literary reputation in France. Garneau's eminence in the early literature of French-speaking Canada ranks with that of Haliburton in Nova Scotia. As a historian, indeed, he has been rated as far surpassing Haliburton. His influence upon the society in which his works appeared and his stimulus on the younger writers of Quebec were profound and sustained.

Among the younger men, quickened by the precept and example of Garneau, the most interesting is Octave Crémazie, the poet.   He caught up the flame from Garneau and spread it ardently.   In Crémazie's life all those contributory influences mentioned elsewhere in this book can be traced: the home, the school, the library, the social club, the intimate circle, the magazine.   Crémazie's family, as I have noted, owned a bookstore in the rue de la Fabrique, in Quebec City. At Laval College, Crémazie came under the influence of a famous educator, a native of Vermont.   In due course he acquired what Wade calls an "astonishing erudition."   Mac-Mechan describes the physical appearance of the not very poetic-looking figure, and comments: "This ugly little book seller was a learned man.   With equal ease he quoted Sophocles and the Ramayana, Juvenal and the Arabian or Scandinavian poets.   He had even studied Sanscrit."[1]

Booksellers both in Quebec and in Montreal provided a kind of informal meeting place which stimulated literary production.   Octave Crémazie's presence in the bookshop owned by his family had unquestionably a catalytic effect on French-Canadian writing.   Louis Fréchette's interest in poetry, it is said, was born there.   Archibald MacMechan has given us a charming sketch of the little book-shop "in the rue de la Fabrique," just opposite the old Jesuit barracks: Crémazie's bookshop, its windows filled with the latest volumes from Paris, was the rendezvous for the best minds in Quebec.   "There Garneau the historian might be seen rubbing elbows with Étienne Parent the thinker, Baron Gauldrée-Boilleau, consul-general for France, shaking hands with Abbé Ferland, while Chaveau turned over the leaves of Pontmartin's *Samedis*.   There LeMay and Fréchette came to read their first essays; there Taché and Cauchon carried on endless arguments, and Gérin-Lajoie loitered after the closing of the legislative library."

[1]MacMechan, Archibald: *Headwaters of Canadian Literature*.   Toronto, 1924.   P. 60.

These associations were not confined to stimulating talk. "With that French instinct for concerted action, so different from English individualism," MacMechan goes on, "this *cénacle* established a magazine, *Les Soirées Canadiennes*, the aim of which is sufficiently indicated by the motto borrowed from Nodier, 'Let us hasten to relate the delightful tales of the people before they have forgotten them.' "[1]

In 1862, a financial indiscretion exiled Crémazie from Quebec to Paris and his days as *Canadien* poet and literary stimulus were virtually over. But from his detached post in the heart of literary Europe he saw the literary struggles of colonial Quebec in a stark light. His subsequent letters to his old friend Abbé Casgrain contain some of the most perceptive observations on pioneer letters we are ever likely to read. These letters, Mason Wade observes, represent the first noteworthy French-Canadian criticism. Crémazie did not allow his patriotic fervour to cloud his judgment. Commenting on Casgrain's enthusiastic summary of the literary movement in Quebec, the critic wrote from Paris:

Mm. Garneau and Ferland, have already, it is true, supplied a granite base for our literary edifice; but if one bird does not make a spring, two books do not constitute a literature. All that has been produced by us, beyond these two great works, seems to me to have no chance of survival. . . . In poetry, in fiction, we have only second-class works. Tragedy, the drama, are still to be born. . . .

As for Canadian writers, it was hopeless for them to expect to earn enough for their least needs, Crémazie wrote. They were placed in the same situation as those of the Middle Ages. Unless they engaged in politics, observed Crémazie—"and God knows the literature that we owe to the tirades of political pundits!"—their pens could not win sufficient for their least needs. The young man leaving college thought it a call to

[1]MacMechan, *op. cit.* P. 61.

the highest destiny to have his name attached to some article in a magazine, Crémazie said, but such foolish vanities of youth soon vanished before the daily cares of life:

The need of gaining his daily bread has imposed upon him the harsh necessity of devoting his life to certain arid occupations, which will blight in him the sweet flowers of the imagination and break the intimate and delicate fibres of poetic sensibility. . . . Under such conditions it is a misfortune to have received from heaven a portion of the divine fire. Since one cannot earn a living by the ideas which boil in one's brain, one must seek employment which is nearly always contrary to one's tastes. The most usual result is that one becomes a bad employee and a bad writer.[1]

How familiar these sentiments are! They run through the story of early Canadian letters like a persistent strain in the minor key. Wilson MacDonald gave the idea a haunting expression in "The Cry of the Song Children," Lloyd Roberts in his moving lyric, "I Would Be Free," and Frederick Philip Grove returned to it again and again.

Crémazie saw penetratingly that if Quebec failed to produce a notable literature in that era, it would not be from lack of talent, but from lack of effective demand. The cause of the inferiority of French-Canadian letters to date lay not in the rarity of men of talent, he wrote, "but in the disastrous environment provided for the writer by the indifference of a population which has as yet no taste for letters, at least for works produced by native sons." It was not that the economy of French-speaking Canada was too poor to support a literature. Mason Wade points out that Crémazie denounced Quebec's "society of grocers." In this he included the professional men with limited vision and oldfashioned tastes. "The masterpieces of foreign literatures were completely unknown and of no concern to them; how should they be

[1]Wade, Mason: *The French Canadians, 1760-1945*. Toronto, 1955. Chapter VI, section 9.

interested in an infant literature?'' Wade quotes Crémazie as observing that in his own bookselling days in Quebec "it was not these pillars of society, but a few students and young priests who bought works of real value and devoted their slim savings to the masterpieces of literature. It seemed to him that there was nothing to do but await better days."[1] Crémazie, of course, would not see it, nor would the contemporaries of Abbé Casgrain at Quebec City, but a brighter day for French-language literature in Canada would nevertheless dawn.

[1]Wade, Mason, *op. cit.* P. 305.

CHAPTER VIII

THE FLOWERING OF FREDERICTON

A PARTICULARLY charming and well-documented episode of English-language letters in Canada is the story of Charles G. D. Roberts, Bliss Carman, Francis Sherman, Theodore Goodridge Roberts, and the lesser literary lights of Fredericton. A creative flame appeared there quite suddenly in the 1880's, burned intensely for a time, duly scattered, and set alight a number of other literary fires, as far apart as Toronto, Ottawa, New York and London. Why this group should appear in this particular part of Canada seems to have baffled some earlier commentators. New Brunswick seemed a sluggish environment to foster such an intense fire; Fredericton at the time of the outburst was a somnolent sylvan capital of less than 6,000 souls, based on lumbering and the Provincial civil service. It was nearly a hundred miles from the Atlantic seaboard, and had been overshadowed from the beginning by the bustling seaport of Saint John. It seemed a much less likely site than Halifax had been for a culmination of cultural activity in the form of important letters. More than one historian has brushed off the phenomenon as a sort of cultural accident or "sport." Closer inquiry into the years of gestation removes much of the mystery connected with the emergence of Roberts, Carman, Sherman and others. Here, too, the foothills preceded the mountains.

There are two or three facts about the Fredericton authors which strike me as being unusual, and as such illuminating. The society which produced them was a tiny and concentrated one, being almost confined to the Bliss's and Roberts's family clan, supplemented by a small urban professional group of clergymen, teachers and lawyers. The quality and intensity of the literary influence within the group must, I think, have compensated for its modest size. And it is worth noting that while the society in which Roberts, Carman and their fellow-writers were reared was able to nurture potential writing genius, it could not provide any economic basis for a continuing literary livelihood: it could ignite, but could not feed, the literary flame. Not a single member of the writing group was ever able to subsist on what Fredericton had to offer, or for that matter on what it could derive from the whole of New Brunswick. Even the most successful man of business in the cluster, Charles G. D. Roberts, owed at the peak of his success as professional man of letters almost nothing in an economic sense to the society in which he had been reared. Other literary flowerings elsewhere have been encouraged and economically sustained by the immediate society in which they have appeared; such could not be said for the Fredericton awakening.

However, it was a rare achievement even to ignite the flame. Alfred G. Bailey, dean of arts at the University of New Brunswick, grandson of one New Brunswick scholar and great-grandson of another, has reported the details of an unusually rich intellectual and cultural society, which flourished for two or three decades before the appearance of *Orion and Other Poems*.

Like the settlers in Nova Scotia, but not, I think, to as great a degree, the early migrants to the Saint John River valley enjoyed some advantages, both of immigrant stock and of environment, over many of the more characteristic interior settlements of pioneer North America. Those frontier communities brought into being by the chance arrival of scattered individuals and isolated families of heterogeneous stock and origin—which was the usual case—would obviously take longer to knit into a society of cohesion and community spirit. The story of Fredericton is not mainly the story of such a settlement. It is true that the United Empire Loyalists who travelled up the Saint John River to the site of the present capital faced for a time physical obstacles of the most challenging nature. But they also enjoyed some of the advantages which helped Windsor, Annapolis Royal, and Halifax to nurture Haliburton and Howe. The Saint John valley was not exactly a howling and untenanted wilderness when the Loyalists came: there had been some pioneer agriculture and forestry, and some scattered areas of village settlement for a long time. Communication with the sea-board was relatively cheap, easy, and fast. Moreover, as in Nova Scotia, the Loyalists came to some extent as a society *en bloc*, and the immigrants included a fair proportion of the same professional classes as helped to settle the Loyalist parts of Nova Scotia. They enjoyed some state assistance in getting settled. There were aristocrats and college graduates among them. And the founders of Fredericton included many families which put great stock in such institutions as the church, the college and the school.

Dr. Bailey recalls that the Loyalists of 1784 had intended the Province to be "the most gentlemanlike in earth," with "a social system patterned on that of contemporary England with its Anglican establishment and control of education, its aristocratic ideal as the guiding principal of the governing

classes, and an agricultural basis to the social pyramid."
Dr. Bailey continues:

> Fredericton became the scene of a belated flowering of the
> Loyalist culture that had stood for class distinctions, gracious
> living, and intellectual cultivation. Jonathan Odell, the
> Tory satirist of the American Revolution, had done much to
> mould the character of the Provincial institutions. Julia
> Catherine Beckwith, the first native-born novelist, had spent
> her formative years in Fredericton. John Medley, the first
> Bishop of Fredericton, was a man of intellectual tastes and
> intellectual distinction. Juliana Horatia Ewing found the
> atmosphere of the little capital congenial.[1]

Educational institutions played such a large part in the
genesis of the literary flowering that the origins are worth
some inquiry. Writing in 1948, as Chief Superintendent of
Education in the Province, Fletcher Peacock recalled that the
year after the founding of the Province, "certain Anglican
Loyalists, some of whom were graduates of Harvard and Yale,
proposed that a block of 6,000 acres in and around Fredericton
be devoted to the maintenance of a 'Provincial Academy of
Arts and Science.' " Esther Clark Wright notes that plans
for such an institution had been laid even before the Loyalists
left New York. Their petition to Governor Carleton was
apparently successful, and once the Colonial Office had
approved the plan, the necessary legislation was passed, and a
provincial charter granted to the "College of New Brunswick"
in 1800.

The ambitions of the university founders met with many
frustrations, but on January 1, 1829, King's College, Fredericton, came into existence, the second institution of that name
in the Maritimes. Thirty years later, after a triumph over
determined popular leaders, who had sought to repeal part of
its charter and lop off its public funds on the grounds that it

[1] *Leading Canadian Poets*, ed. W. P. Percival, Toronto, 1948, p 194; see
also, A. G. Bailey, *Dalhousie Review*, October 1949, pp 239-244.

was essentially an Anglican divinity school, it became, by Act of the Legislature, the University of New Brunswick. Meantime, in a series of changes of name and charter, the predecessor of the Fredericton High School of the 1880's survived first as The Academy, then as the Grammar School and finally as the Collegiate School of the University. If one seeks the cultural ancestry of such writers as Charles G. D. Roberts and Bliss Carman, it is necessary to consider the scholarship and stimulation of both these institutions of learning, as well as the social heredity of Fredericton itself and the family ancestry of the Roberts and Carman group.

Not everyone will accept the interpretation of Dr. Bailey, that the Fredericton of Roberts's formative years was, in essence, a belated flowering of Loyalist culture. Ninety years of exile and dilution and admixture, ninety years of the pervasive influence of the New Brunswick farm and forest setting, might be thought to be fatal to all but the most tenacious of Loyalist traditions and hereditary strands. The intellectual and literary forces at work in Fredericton in the 1870's were a complex of many sources. The flowering owed a great deal to Oxford.

No doubt the New England strain played a considerable part, however. Jonathan Odell has been mentioned. Called by an American literary historian "by far the best of the Tory satirists," he was one of the founders of the educational institution that grew into the Provincial university. Charles G. D. Roberts, Bliss Carman and Barry Straton could all trace, on their mother's side, a family relationship with the poet Ralph Waldo Emerson. But Roberts was descended, too, on his father's side, from a long line of English scholars. Both his grandfather and his great-grandfather were graduates of Oxford, and his father was a fine classical scholar. In other branches of his father's family, the Goodridges and Gostwyckes, Charles G. D. could trace figures prominent in

English scholastic literary life. Without attempting to assess the role of biological inheritance, we can assume that with a family tradition of this sort on both sides of the house, the climate of spiritual values in which the Roberts children were raised would be of a special and distinctive kind. The inducements toward a life of scholarship, of literary attainment of professional prestige, would be unusually strong.

The leading members of the Fredericton Group were all educated at the Collegiate School, and went on to the University of New Brunswick. A search for cultural catalysts and stimulators in these institutions turns up some interesting facts. It is not possible to assess the precise significance of any one, but they add up into an impressive total. Professor Alfred G. Bailey, whose grandfather joined the faculty of the University of New Brunswick shortly after its creation as an expanded non-sectarian college, singles out J. Marshal d'Avray, a Jerseyman of French descent, as a pioneer in the awakening of Fredericton's scholastic and literary life. "Already in 1848," he writes, "Baron d'Avray had founded the first Provincial normal school, and as newspaper editor, chief superintendent of education, and professor of modern languages at the University he gave an impetus to scholarship that bore fruit in the creative achievements of the poets. Sir George Parkin and the father of Sir Charles G. D. Roberts, to whom the poets acknowledged their greatest debt, were among his students in English and French literature. His romantic background, his fresh and vigorous English, his fine sense of what was the best in the literature of Europe, and his "charming dry wit" were sources of inspiration that these men handed on to their successors. He was one of a distinguished company that included some of the greatest teachers in the history of a Province where teaching was practised as an art."[1]

It is clear, from Bailey and other sources, that the cultured

[1]Bailey, *Dalhousie Review*.   Article cited, p. 242.

atmosphere in which Roberts, Carman, Sherman and others throve, had been long in the making, some of it dating back long before they were born, some of it most active in the years while they were small children.

The outstanding influence of George Parkin on Roberts and Carman has been frequently noted, and it cannot be ignored here. Parkin became headmaster of the Collegiate School in 1871, when he was twenty-five. What he owed to Baron d'Avray has been indicated. He succeeded, as Headmaster, Dr. George Roberts, the grandfather of Charles G. D. Roberts. Parkin was thus following in the footsteps of no routine or mediocre pedagogue. Dr. George Roberts had held the post for thirty-four years, and he had resigned only to accept the post of Professor of Greek at the University of New Brunswick. Dr. Roberts was a distinguished graduate of Oxford, and a fine classical scholar. Is it not a reasonable inference that Parkin, a New Brunswick village boy recently graduated with a bachelor's degree from the University of New Brunswick, felt himself somewhat inadequately equipped to fill the Oxford scholar's giant shoes? At any rate, two years later, in 1873, we find Parkin leaving Fredericton for a year at the great English seat of learning. The political crusades of Parkin's later career may have somewhat obscured the fact that his sojourn at Oxford also kindled in him a passionate love of the English poets. While there, also, he came much under the influence of Ruskin. Before he returned he made a tour of Italy. Then he came back to resume his duties at the Collegiate School at Fredericton, where Charles Roberts, a boy of fourteen, was in his classes. So was Bliss Carman, then twelve, and, a little later, Francis Sherman and Theodore Goodridge Roberts.

It is not necessary to guess about the literary influence of George Parkin upon Roberts and Bliss Carman, because both of them have left eloquent and touching tribute. E. M.

Pomeroy, the biographer of Roberts, singles out Parkin's influence as outstanding in those years, regarded by Roberts afterwards indeed as second only to that of his father. "Like all great teachers," writes Miss Pomeroy, "Parkin was the vital enthusiast who knew each member of his class and was interested in each one individually. His subjects were English and the classics, and there was none of the dry classroom method in his presentation of the great classical poetry. In his rich and sonorous voice he read passages from Homer, Virgil and Horace, not academically as if they were merely subjects for scansion, but rhythmically and lyrically, so that they were as obviously poetry to the ears of his students as passages from Keats and Shelley."[1]

A few months after Bliss Carman's death, Charles G. D. Roberts wrote a memoir for *The Dalhousie Review* in which he expanded on this subject:

It was outside school hours that Parkin did most for us two ardent boys,—that he gave us most inspiringly of himself, of his high enthusiasms, and of the atmosphere of that wonderful far world of art and letters from which he had just returned. Filling our pockets with apples . . . he would take us favoured two for long hikes over the wooded hills behind Fredericton. He would take us as comrades, not as pupils; and his talk would weave magic for us till the austere fir-clad slopes would transform themselves before us into the soft green Cumnor Hills, and the roofs and spires of Fredericton, far below, would seem to us the ivied towers of Oxford. England just then was thrilling to the new music, the new colour, the new raptures of Swinburne and Rossetti; Parkin was steeped in them; and in his rich voice he would recite to us ecstatically, over and over till we too were intoxicated with them, the great choruses from "Atlanta in Calydon," passages from "The Triumph of Time," and "Rococo,"—but above all, "The Blessed Damozel," which he loved so passionately that Bliss suspected him of sometimes saying it instead of his prayers. But Parkin's love and understanding of poetry was not con-

[1]Pomeroy, E. M.: *Sir Charles G. D. Roberts.* Toronto, 1943. Pp. 20-21.

fined to the work of the Pre-Raphaelite group. He would
quote Tennyson, Browning and Arnold to us; and he taught us
to know Homer and Horace, not as subjects for laborious
translation and scansion and parsing, but as supreme poets
and masters of verbal music.   In conversation with us, indeed,
he was given to quoting from Horace as familiarly as from the
English poets.[1]

Miss Pomeroy adds that the influence of Parkin persisted,
and that Roberts himself would quote passages from Homer
and Horace with the same note of exaltation as he recited the
poetry of his beloved Keats and Shelley.   When Roberts was
graduated from the College School at sixteen, it was as
winner of the Douglas Gold Medal in classics.

Carman sat at Parkin's feet at a younger and still more
impressionable age, and stayed with him longer, and it is
probable that Parkin's influence on Carman was even greater
than that on Roberts.   In a letter which R. H. Hathaway
wrote to Bliss Carman on September 20, 1921, there appears
this revealing paragraph:

"By the way, Sir George Parkin is in town just now, and
has been much interested in my collection of your work.
He has a very vivid memory of the time when you were a lad
under him, and recalled your coming to him *with your very
first verses.*"

Carman related his indebtedness to Parkin on more than
one occasion.   His dedication to him of the book of essays,
The Kinship of Nature (published 1903) reads as follows:

The service you did him (Carman) is, next to the gift of life,
the greatest thing that one man can render another.

Those were the days when we were all young together,
whether at Greek or football, tramping for Mayflowers through
the early spring woods, paddling on the river in intoxicating
Junes, or snowshoeing across bitter drifts in the perishing
December wind—always under the leadership of your

[1]Pomeroy, *op. cit.*   Pp. 21-22.

indomitable ardour.   In that golden age we first realized the
kinship of Nature, whose help is for ever unfailing, and whose
praise is never outsung.   I must remind you, too, of those
hours in the classroom, when the Aeneid was often interrupted
by the *Idylls of the King* or *The Blessed Damozel*, and William
Morris or Arnold or Mr. Swinburne's latest lyric came to us
between the lines of Horace.

We are told that Bliss Carman first met Parkin in the home
of Loring Woart Bailey, Professor of Science at the University,
a graduate of Harvard and a student of Agassiz.   Concerning
this meeting, Carman afterwards wrote: "I did not guess that
I was to come under his care some years later, to spend six of
the most impressionable years of my life under his daily
supervision and guidance; and to become forever indebted
to him more than anyone else except my parents for the most
precious things of life."

Carman returned again and again to the theme of his
indebtedness.   Since much has been made in earlier pages of
the role played by the teacher in stimulating literary creation,
I must risk a charge of over-emphasizing Parkin's influence on
Carman by quoting another tribute:

I cannot conceive of a teacher with greater power to arouse
and inspire his pupils than Dr. Parkin had—a power he possessed in such abundance and spent so lavishly. . . . The
Collegiate School had traditions of its own, an honourable
history behind it, and a pride in its past which its new head-
master was careful to foster. . . . He was a fascinating
teacher, this intense and magnetic personality. . . . In the
classics, which were his chief subjects, his great appreciation of
poetry and letters gave unusual scope to the day's work.
With him as instructor, it was impossible not to feel the beauty
of Virgil's lovely passages and the greatness of Homer as he
read them. . . . A reference might occur which would bring
up a side issue in history or mythology, and then we must see
how some modern or contemporary writer had treated the
same theme.   One of the class would be sent running to

Parkin's rooms to fetch a book; Tennyson, perhaps, or Rossetti, or Arnold, or another, and we must listen to his poem on the subject. There were wonderful hours of growth, though we never dreamed of our incomparable good fortune, so rare a tutor. I can hear now that ringing voice in many lines of English poetry, as he read them to us, feeling all their glorious beauty. Small wonder if some of us became infected with the rhythm of the Muses, all unconsciously, and must be haunted for ever by the cadence of golden words.[1]

When Roberts and Carman had completed their studies at the Collegiate School, they enrolled in the University, Roberts in the autumn of 1876, Carman two years later. Dr. George E. Foster (later Sir George) was professor of classics, and Dr. Thomas Harrison Professor of English, Philosophy, and Economics. Classics was Roberts's favourite subject at college, but Dr. Harrison was the teacher to whom he seems to have owed most during his college years. Foster, like Parkin, came out of the New Brunswick village and country environment, and, like Parkin, he had supplemented his Fredericton University education with studies abroad. Foster returned from Edinburgh and Heidelberg in 1873. When Roberts entered the University in 1876, Foster was thirty-nine. Dr. Thomas Harrison was another product of the New Brunswick village. He had crossed the Atlantic to study at Trinity College, Dublin, and at the University of Dublin. He had shone at Mathematics while at College, and had acquired the degrees of Bachelor and then Doctor of Laws, as well as Bachelor and Master of Arts.

It is clear from these and other considerations that academic New Brunswick could not have been quite the "sterile soil" referred to by Professor Lower as being the seedbed of the Roberts-Carman group. The comments of Professor Pelham Edgar to the effect that the staffs of Collegiate School and University "were not noteworthy in the scholarly sense" and

[1]Willison, Sir John S.: *Sir George Parkin*. London, 1929. Pp. 35-36.

his assumption that "the standards were not, on a comparative estimate, high," are equally open to challenge.   Whatever the comparative excellence of Parkin, Foster, Bailey and Harrison may have been, these men brought to Fredericton intellectual fire and emotional life caught up in such rich and varied contacts as Harvard, Trinity College, Oxford, Edinburgh and Heidelberg, and from such personalities as Agassiz, Ruskin, Nettleship (a Virgil scholar) and H. H. Asquith, who was president of the Oxford Union at the time when Parkin was its secretary.   When one adds in the classical tradition of the Roberts family and its family heritage of Oxford, one is led to the conviction that the Fredericton seedbed was much richer than has been supposed.   Where, indeed, at the time, was there anything in Canada anything like as good?

When Roberts began to compose poetry in his first year at College, Fredericton, as I have said, was a quiet Provincial capital of about 6,000 inhabitants.   Saint John, the chief city of New Brunswick, held about 35,000.   The cultural soil of the region was evidently capable of *breeding* poets, essayists and novelists, as events proved: but the Provincial society was quite unable to offer an economic market for even the most modest production of *belles lettres*.   The work of Roberts and his relatives, of Bliss Carman, Francis Sherman, and Barry Straton had to find, for the most part, commercial sale elsewhere.   New Brunswick in 1880 was obviously a much poorer local market for literature than Nova Scotia had been fifty years earlier.   One favourable circumstance, however, was that in the intervening half century communications with Ontario and Quebec (with which New Brunswick and Nova Scotia were now bound in federal union) and with New York and New England had materially improved.   The railway and the steamship linked all the great centres.   Fredericton and other Maritime cities were now connected with the growth of central Canada, and of Boston and Philadelphia and other

American cities. Much has been made of the economic disadvantage under which Canadian authors have always suffered because of competition from the cheaper wares of Britain and the United States. But another and more attractive side of the matter should not be forgotten. A Canadian is not confined to his own country in marketing his manuscripts. Writing in English, he can sell to the whole English-speaking world. The value of this immensely larger market was clearly evident in the literary history of Roberts, and later of Bliss Carman and other members of the Fredericton Group. In the end, of course, an important native literature must have a printing and publishing and distributing industry on its own soil.

The earliest of Roberts's published poems appeared, as has been said, in a short-lived magazine published in Montreal. When Roberts was seventeen, he wrote a poem entitled "Memnon," which was accepted by Scribner's *Monthly*, and appeared in June, 1879. Two other poems, "Ariadne" and "An Ode to Drowsihood," written soon after "Memnon," appeared in the same magazine. As I have mentioned, in 1879, when Roberts was nineteen, he brought together a collection of college verse which he called *Orion and Other Poems*. Modest enough in size, and limited perhaps even in intrinsic poetic merit, it was still a historic volume in terms of its influence on Canadian literature. The circumstances of its publication are interesting, not the least for the fact that they provide a small link between the Howe-Haliburton period in Halifax and the early creative years of Fredericton.

The Queen's Printer of New Brunswick in 1879 was George E. Fenety. Fenety was a native of Halifax, who at the age of seventeen, in 1829, had entered Joseph Howe's office, and had there begun his newspaper career. Six years later he had gone to New York, and later to Donaldsville, on the Mississippi, where he published the *Planters' Advocate*.

By 1839, he was back in British North America, founding at Saint John the *Commercial News*, a thrice-weekly newspaper said to have been the first penny paper published in the Maritimes. He edited this newspaper for twenty-four years. He was then appointed Queen's Printer for New Brunswick and moved to Fredericton.

In such a small community it was only to be expected that an ambitious young writer like Charles Roberts would be drawn to this influential printer and publisher, and veteran newsman. To be sure, there were attractions other than literary in the Fenety household. Before Charles graduated from the University of New Brunswick he was engaged to Fenety's "shy and extremely pretty" daughter, Mary. Subsequently, in December, 1880, they were married. One is not surprised to learn that when Roberts had a manuscript of poems ready for a publisher he should first consult the best authority in Fredericton; what was not so inevitable was that the crusty, hard-headed old Queen's Printer should be moved to find the necessary cash to guarantee publication of *Orion and Other Poems*.

The influence of this collection of poems on Lampman and other Ontario students will be noticed later. Roberts was proud enough of his achievement to send copies to six poets of international reputation, and he won as reward for his audacity long letters of commendation and encouragement from Matthew Arnold and Oliver Wendell Holmes, both of whom he met in later years.

When *Orion and Other Poems* appeared, Roberts was head-master of the Grammar School at Chatham. At the end of January, 1882, when Roberts had just turned twenty-two, he moved back to Fredericton to be principal of the York Street School. The correspondence with his cousin Bliss Carman in this period illustrates the role he played as "big brother," stimulator and critic of Carman's early poetry. In his ambition to get ahead, Roberts was stealing every possible hour out of his loaded teaching week to contribute to the magazines, to prepare academic addresses, to write such articles as that on New Brunswick for *Picturesque Canada*, and, if any shred of energy was still left, to compose poetry. His contributions to Goldwin Smith's *Bystander* and the reputation he had acquired through the publication of *Orion and Other Poems* led to an invitation to come up to Toronto to edit a new publication then being planned by Goldwin Smith. His stay in Ontario on that occasion was destined to be brief, but his influence on the literary movement in central Canada considerable. This will be examined briefly in the next chapter.

Since this is a study of the frontier and pioneer aspects of Canadian letters it would be out of place to attempt either an estimate of the literary achievement of the Fredericton Group or a recital of their later fortunes. But the latter would throw, by implication, some light on the current state of Canadian literary activity, and a few words are needed here.

Charles G. D. Roberts, Bliss Carman, Theodore Goodridge Roberts and William Carman Roberts all aspired to be full-time professional men of letters in one field or another. All of them found it necessary to leave Canada in order to become so. Francis Sherman was an amateur poet of real distinction, but never thought of poetry as a means of livelihood. He became a successful banker, and his poetic output had essentially ended by the time he was twenty-nine. Barry Straton, Elizabeth Roberts MacDonald, and Lloyd Roberts—except for a brief stay in New York—remained in Canada and wrote when they could.

The influence of the Fredericton Group of writers on Canadian letters was widespread and lasting. The effect of *Orion and Other Poems* on Archibald Lampman is noticed later. T. G. Marquis, writing years afterwards in *The Canadian*

Magazine, paid tribute to the influence of Charles G. D. Roberts as a teacher at Chatham:

> His influence over the minds of the elder pupils was very great, and the hour of his arrival gave some of us our bent. From that hour we loved literature, to one among us it became a passion that even a residence in flat, unpoetic, grain-growing cheese-producing Ontario cannot eradicate.

Roberts spent ten years at King's College, Windsor, and there his influence radiated out from the classroom into a wider community. One agency for the contagion of literary passion was the Haliburton Club there, of which Roberts became president when he arrived, holding the office for ten years. The aims of the club were defined as follows: "It was the outcome of a desire on the part of certain leading graduates and undergraduates to further in some degree the development of a distinctive literature in Canada. As a tributary to this aim the founders proposed the collection of Canadian books and manuscripts and of works bearing on our history and literature."

Douglas Sladen, writing in 1895, told of a visit to King's College, noting there among the undergraduates "a genuine regard for poetry, which has resulted in a more literary atmosphere than I ever remember finding in a university."[1]

The novelist H. A. Cody, Venerable Archdeacon and Rector of St. James Church, Saint John, and Robert Norwood, Canadian poet and onetime Rector of St. Bartholomew's Church, New York City, have both testified to his stimulating influence on his students. At a King's College Reunion in 1930, Robert Norwood said: "My success in life is due to Charles Roberts. Roberts has not only ennobled Canadian literature, but has made Canadians realize its nobility."[2]

---

[1] *On the Cars and Off.* New York, 1895.
[2] Pomeroy, *op. cit.* P. 65.

It would be possible to amplify at length this brief reference to the influence of the Fredericton Group. It was not confined to the Maritime Provinces. If a personal tribute is not out of place here, this book would never have been attempted if an eight-year-old boy, in a "little white schoolhouse" within sight of the Alberta Foothills, had not found in the rural school library a copy of *Kindred of the Wild*, and had not, a bit later, discovered in a copy of a farm magazine one of the haunting lyrics of Bliss Carman.

Of all the Fredericton Group, Roberts was the leader and central influence. Generous tribute to his achievement was paid by Lorne Pierce, in his introduction to the biography by Elsie M. Pomeroy:

He was the first poet . . . deliberately to break with the old world tradition, and consciously and continuously set himself to be the spokesman and interpreter of his own country. He was the first to rally a whole choir of native song, give it centre and meaning, and inspire it for half a century, until the last sceptic about a Canadian literature had disappeared. He was the first, with *Orion*, to challenge once and for all the writers of the old world, and announce that voices in the new Dominion could sing songs in a new way. . . . He was the first of the popular historians of Canada who joined style to matter, and gave the nation the first account of its life that aroused pride in its past and pride in its assured destiny. He was the first to write successful travel literature, turning the feet of the tourist toward our historic places. He was the first successful translator of French-Canadian fiction into English, and the first literary champion of the *bonne entente* between our two great races. . . . He was the first to establish a literary movement and remained at its head for two generations. . . .[1]

[1]Pomeroy, *op. cit.*   Pp. xxii-xxiii.

CHAPTER IX

FRONTIER VALUES OUTLIVE
THE FRONTIER

BY 1867 THE advancing farm frontier of central Canada had pushed up against the rock and pine of the Precambrian Shield. All the good land was already occupied. But the typical frontier values persisted. Ontario society was singularly slow to produce a climate and soil favourable to the growth of native arts and letters. It may be useful to speculate on the reasons. Also, some preparation was made for later flowerings, and a few isolated literary figures of real merit emerged. It seems worth while to carry the survey along to the end of the century.

Confederation promised a more exciting future for the people of Canada West. Federal union had rescued them from a political impasse. Statesmen like George Brown saw in the North-West a vast extension of the Province and a wealthy hinterland for the Provincial industries. Meantime the Intercolonial Railway would open up the markets of the Maritimes. There was a new spirit of national excitement in the air. The first eight or nine years of Dominion status brought high hopes to the Canadian people.   Lofty sentiments of empire building excited the imagination: and the new mood was reflected in cultural and literary vitality.   In his excellent study of this period, Alfred G. Bailey cites evidence of a hopeful spirit among Canadian writers and editors.[1]   *The Canadian Monthly* in 1873 drew from an English journalist a tribute to the "important native literature springing up in the country" and an assertion that this was "the most vigorous of colonial literary productions . . . quite able to stand side by side with our home produce."   In 1875, Dr. Bailey says, the editor of *The Nation* "modestly put forward Toronto's claim to be the literary capital of the Dominion."   The editor of *The Canadian Monthly*, when launching his magazine, felt that conditions in Canada began to justify such a venture. "The range of studies," Dr. Bailey quotes him as saying, "has grown wider and the taste is becoming critical, if not fastidious.   There is an evident desire to keep up with the knowledge of the time and . . . for the latest and noblest fruits of contemporary intellect."

Unhappily this exalted mood did not last.   After 1875 economic conditions became adverse.   As it turned out, the "Great Depression" had begun and was not to lift for twenty years.   Economic stagnation followed, and hard times were accompanied by national bickering.   Relations between the two great races of Canada soured.   By 1891 the mood was such that Wilfrid Laurier could write gloomily to Edward Blake that the premature dissolution of the Dominion seemed to be at hand.   It was not really until the turn of the century, by which time a number of national and international factors had changed for the better, that the vibrant faith of the early 1870's was recaptured.

This ebb and flow of national feeling, and of Canadian

[1]"Literature and Nationalism After Confederation," *University of Toronto Quarterly*, July, 1956.   Pp. 409-424.

prosperity, was reflected in cultural affairs. When the early promise was not fulfilled, many ambitious authors turned their eyes to other lands. The "Golden Age" remained a mirage: few native writers appeared; those who did met a harsh cultural climate. Examination of the literature produced between 1867 and 1900 is a disappointment. Set aside the *émigré* writers, and the later work of expatriates, and there is little of merit left. Nor was the public's treatment of those few authentic and gifted authors who elected to remain in Canada such as to suggest a congenial or appreciative society. Quite the contrary, in fact. Principal "Geordie" Grant of Queen's, addressing the Royal Society in 1891, said that Section II of the Society, that devoted to literary and historical studies, had been from its birth in a condition of anaemia. Robert Barr, as late as 1900, wrote bitterly that "Canada is about the poorest book market in the world outside Senegambia." Such observations could be matched from many sources.

Foundations were being laid, of course, but little had yet appeared above the surface. Those cultural prerequisites stressed in earlier chapters were gradually emerging. Institutions of higher learning were by now well established in such centres as Toronto, Kingston and Cobourg. A series of magazines of a literary and scientific nature appeared, flourished briefly, but then disappeared. The Canadian Institute had been started in 1849. Printing and publishing were on their way to becoming an important industry in Toronto, heralding the day when that city would become without question the literary capital of English-speaking Canada, and one of the main forces in the fostering of native letters.

The unsatisfactory position of having to depend on foreign publishers was spelled out by E. W. Thomson in 1891, in a letter to Wilfred Campbell. "The American magazines," he wrote, "steadily refuse my Bransby sketch, as 'too long for a magazine' or 'too local in interest,' always with some objection that I recognize as not unjust. We Canadians are a good deal hampered by the lack of literary publications in our own country, for, in appealing, by fiction, to foreign audiences we are required not only to drop out much racy of the soil and to refrain from merely allusive remarks that would be instantly understood in Canada, but also to place ourselves mentally in the place of the foreign reader. It is writing in hobbles."[1]

It would not be fair to leave the impression that the Canadian periodical did nothing for the budding author of the times. William Kirby's first verse appeared in the *Niagara Chronicle*. Some of Isabella Valancy Crawford's first poems were printed in *The Globe*. Lampman's first literary paper appeared in *Rouge et Noir*, the college publication, while he was still an undergraduate at Trinity University. *The Varsity* printed the first verse of William Wilfred Campbell. Such literary and intellectual periodicals as *The Canadian Monthly*, *The Nation*, Belford's *Monthly* and *The Canadian Magazine* stimulated Canadian writing and raised the intellectual temperature of the Province. The special contribution of Goldwin Smith's *The Week* is noticed in another place.

But without detracting from the credit due to the editors of periodicals in the development of a native literature, it should be stressed that a newspaper or magazine press of itself was never likely to foster an important literature. The book is indispensable for a literary blossoming. It was unrealistic to expect a vigorous Canadian literature until such time as at least one strong book-printing and publishing centre should be established, with adequate facilities for the importing, export-ing and distribution of books on a substantial scale. As it

[1]Quoted in the letters of Archibald Lampman to E. W. Thomson, edited by Arthur Bourinot, Ottawa, 1956.   P. 65.

turned out, Toronto was destined (for English-speaking Canada) to become that centre. How important it might ultimately become would obviously depend a good deal on the appetite for fine literature among the Canadian people, and on the competition from the outside. At least it can be reported that it was during the years from 1867 to 1900 that Toronto began to lay the foundations for its future role as literary capital.

The insistence on a native printing and publishing industry may seem to some overdrawn. Was it not possible to go a long way toward an important Canadian literature while still calling on the resources of London, Paris, Boston and New York? The Howe-Haliburton output had, it is true, been achieved without much more in the way of native industry than the presses of *The Novascotian* and the personal drive of Joseph Howe as publisher and distributor. The brief literary flowering of New Brunswick was achieved in the virtual absence of a New Brunswick press. But both of these were creative "*moments*," they were not as it proved the forerunners of an established native literature. So long as any country has to rely on the publishers, printers and booksellers of other lands to bring its native authorship to fruition, it is not likely to attain either literary eminence or continuity.

This may be the most convenient point at which to consider the story of British North American printing in brief perspective.

Through the indefatigable industry of Marie Tremaine, we have an exhaustive account of British North American imprints for the years 1751 to 1800. The first French settlements along the St. Lawrence and in the Maritime region of Acadia were established many decades earlier, yet so far as can be established not a single book was printed in New France before the Conquest. The first press was that of Bartholomew Green, Jr., of Halifax in 1751. A total of

sixteen printing offices had been opened in British North
America by the end of the eighteenth century; nine of these
were still functioning in 1800.   The output was almost exclusively official, or utilitarian in some way.   Canadian printers
found that almanacs were a profitable staple.   Most of the
early presses were operated by a King's or Queen's Printer,
whose mainstay was the official work of publishing laws,
proclamations, speeches, notices and government advertising.
Another early staple in North America was school text books,
especially in the French-speaking areas.   Religious works,
chiefly Catholic, were produced in quantity.

As for *belles lettres*, the chief concern of this examination,
the era before 1800 was almost completely blank.   Marie
Tremaine disposes of the subject in a few lines:

Poetry, drama, and *belles lettres* appeared hardly at all
from the earliest Canadian presses.   Two poems, indeed, were
printed in pamphlet form in Quebec, apparently in small
editions for their authors, but both are remarkable for their
then fashionable style than for poetic significance.   Another,
Annapolis Royal, a country clergyman's tribute to a beautiful
valley, has an awkward gait, but expresses a feeling for the
region that Canadians of a later generation recognize with
sympathetic understanding.   Plans to publish collected
editions of the poems of local amateurs and of a European
best-seller, Robert Burns, alike failed for lack of support.

Such is the whole Canadian story up to 1800.[1]

The production of books in the days before the invention
of the linotype or similar type-setting machines was tedious
and complicated.   To set up a whole book at once required
enormous quantities of expensive type—resources far beyond
the modest means of most pioneer printers.   Their custom was
to set a few pages, print sheets, and then break up the forms

[1]Tremaine, Marie: *A Bibliography of Canadian Imprints*.   Toronto, 1952.
Pp. xi-xx.

and use the same type again—for additional pages of the book, or for other more urgent work, such as a weekly *Gazette*. Under these circumstances full-length book production was rare, even after printing presses had been widely established in British North America. Colonial records show that some books took four years to print.

The first book production in Toronto on any sustained basis seems to have been sponsored by the Methodist Church. In 1829, Egerton Ryerson was given permission to purchase a printing press primarily for the publication of Methodist tracts, sermons and papers. The first big printing job undertaken by the "Methodist Book Room" was Everett's *Life of Sammy Hick, the Village Blacksmith* (1835). The first travel book was published in 1855.[1] The history of Toronto written by Professor D. C. Masters discloses no evidence of material book publication before the "Great Boom Period" of 1867-1875. "The literature and art of Toronto," he says of that era, "were still largely derivative, although, as in the preceding period, some slight signs of emancipation appeared. The book notices were still almost completely of American and British publications. Canadian editions were, however, being published by Copp Clark and Company, and Adam, Stevenson and Company. Toronto was, therefore, acquiring the means of publishing indigenous literature when it developed." A decade later, "a single forerunner of an age of native production appeared . . . with the publication of William Kirby's *Golden Dog*. Although printed in Montreal and New York, it was advertised in Toronto in 1877 and may perhaps be regarded as representing some slight development in the direction of the taste for a native literature."[2]

Henry J. Morgan says that the firm of Hunter, Rose and Co., which had the contract for government printing at

[1]See *The House of Ryerson*, by Lorne Pierce, Toronto, 1954.
[2]Masters, D. C.: *The Rise of Toronto*. Toronto, 1947.

Ottawa, began after 1865 to devote some attention to the publication o fiction and school books. They opened a branch for his purpose in Toronto, and in 1871 transferred all their operations to that city. They then entered extensively into the business of publishing Canadian reprints of English copyrighted books, "principally the popular novels of living writers, for which a ready market was found." Hunter, Rose and Co. also published for a time the *Canadian Monthly* and what Morgan calls the *Rose-Belford Magazine*.

As late as 1890, according to George Glazebrook, Canadians read the books of Britain, France and the United States. Such publishing houses as had been established by that date "were mainly concerned with the effort to publish British books in Canada, and here they had to compete with overwhelming American competition." Perhaps 1890 may be taken as a turning point for the better. By then, The Ryerson Press was on the eve of a period of important expansion: its authors' lists in the 1890's included William Kirby, Frederick George Scott, William Wilfred Campbell and Charles G. D. Roberts. After the turn of the century progress continued, though as late as 1914, according to Elizabeth Hay Trott, Canadian publishing did not exceed fifteen per cent of the total sales in Canada, and this was mainly of an educational or religious character. Only after 1922 did Canadian book publishing become an important industry; and only after 1940 was the development spectacular. By 1952 there were seventy-four publishing houses in Canada, including sixteen producing works in French.[1]

This brief summary suggests that for over 150 years after the first English settlements on the Nova Scotia coast, Canadian authors still lacked a book publishing industry capable of co-operating vigorously with them toward the creation of an important Canadian literature.

[1] Article in *The Monetary Times*, June, 1952.

A book-making industry, of course, while essential, is still not enough. The publisher must be much more than another manufacturer. Lorne Pierce writes:

Publishers have been renowned explorers. They have all been born with an instinct for high adventure. No nook or cranny of the world, but, sooner or later, will have seen these adventurers questing for writers, those whose words had so much life in them that they defied death. Upon these they have lavished their high art, squandering time and treasure and all their strength if so be that everyone might know of them. Best of all, they have shown great pride in their own lands, whether proud kingdom or humble city state, and they have urged artists and writers unceasingly to paint and sing and write what they saw of the life crowding about them. They have implored these creative spirits to give some true hint of the wealth hidden in their native soil, to explain their own people to themselves and be their spokesmen to the world. Every nation that has ever reached maturity has had these master builders working for it, and not infrequently these have been the real first ministers of the realm.[1]

Publishers of this quality and spirit were slow to appear in Canada. Until they did it was idle to look for a strong native literature.

It is now time to turn to the Ontario authors of the period under survey. The first impression is less of group or society activity—a true flowering of an integrated cultural community—than of a stubborn upthrust of a few scattered and almost incidental or accidental artists into a mainly hostile or indifferent environment. The body   work to be considered depends a lot on definition.

The novelist who won highest acclaim, William Kirby, was already in his twenties before he settled in Canada. The poetess most admired today came from Ireland as a girl; she owed a great deal to an older culture; moreover she won

[1]Pierce, Lorne: *On Publishers and Publishing*. Toronto, 1951. P. 2.

scant recognition from contemporary Ontario society. The
two Ontario poets of unquestioned eminence to emerge in the
nineteenth century, Lampman and Scott, owed little to the
larger society in which they lived. They brought out books of
verse at their own expense, and for their recognition as poets
they had to depend mainly on magazine editors in the United
States. George Frederick Cameron was a Maritimer who
had reached the age of twenty-eight before he took up
residence in Ontario. Gilbert Parker left Canada for
Australia shortly after graduation, and then went to England.
Peter McArthur departed to make a living in New York, when
he was twenty-four; later he went to London. E. W. Thomson left Canada for Boston in 1891. Sarah Duncan wrote her
stories of Canadian life in far-off India. Robert Barr was a
native of Glasgow who came to Canada at the age of five and
left it forever when he was twenty-six. The list trails off into
names that mean nothing to the average Canadian of today
and very little even to the student of Canadian letters. We
are left with a corporal's guard: Mair, Lampman, Scott,
Campbell, and possibly Pauline Johnson. Even if the region
under consideration were extended to English-speaking
Quebec, it would only be necessary to add Frederick
George Scott and W. H. Drummond. Not an imposing
cluster for the first generation of central Canadian writers
after Confederation!

With the larger society of Ontario so indifferent, what
nurtured even this small cluster? The answer seems to lie
in family influences, supplemented by cultural stimuli brought
in from the outside world, specifically by Goldwin Smith and
Charles G. D. Roberts, the latter carrying a literary spark
from the flame recently ignited at Fredericton.

The childhood of Charles Mair, spent in a village recently
carved out of the primitive forest, supplies evidence of the
value in the early days of effective parental links with the

larger literary world overseas. Mair was born in Lanark, Upper Canada, in 1839, the son of a lumberman. Lanark was then less than two decades old: it was described as "a thriving village" of about 500 souls. There could have been little in this Upper Canada settlement favourable to the moulding of a literary figure, outside the home of the Mairs themselves. Mair's mother was born in Scotland of English descent. Her father, a Mr. Holmes, was a lover of good literature and a great admirer of Sir Walter Scott. Of his mother, Mair wrote: "She was a great reader, loved poetry; and had an inborn instinct for good literature. These traits continued after the family emigrated to Canada, where I, her youngest, was born."

Asked from whom he had inherited his love of books and his poetical talent, Mair once answered, in some detail:

From my mother, no doubt. My father was a highly intelligent man of affairs, but my mother was very fond of poetry and well read in it. After the fairy tales of childhood, she gave me Spenser's *Faerie Queen* in Charles Knight's excellent edition for a boy, in which the finest stanzas were connected by descriptive prose, and never wearied me. . . . My father had a well-chosen library, took *Blackwood's*, the Quarterlies, and *Punch*, also our own *Literary Garland* . . . and an admirably edited newspaper, The New York *Albion*, delightfully British, but the Yankees would not allow it to live! When old enough I read a great deal in general literature: Chaucer's *Canterbury Tales*, Malory's imperishable *Morte D'Arthur*, Chapman's *Odyssey*, and a great many of Shakespeare's Dramas. . . .[1]

Mair read Mrs. Moodie's poems and stories as a boy, and saw what could be done with the Canadian scene.

The importance of the teacher has been stressed earlier. Mair paid tribute to the debt he owed to the Scottish dominie in the village of Perth. Still more valuable to him was the influence of John Macintyre, the principal of the High School,

[1] *Tecumseh, A Drama, Etc.*   Toronto, 1926.   P. lv.

"an accomplished scholar and graduate of Queen's, whose knowledge of literature was comprehensive: and he it was who introduced me to the English classics."

Archibald Lampman's home life could hardly have been more stimulating for a budding poet. Duncan Campbell Scott recalls that Lampman dedicated the volume *Alcyone*: "To my father who first instructed me in the art of verse." Scott adds that "the father was able to instruct by example; he had a gift for versification and a true delight in poetry." It was fortunate for Archibald Lampman that music and poetry were so highly regarded in his home, since, as Scott says, "beyond that home influence there was little or nothing in the Canada of that day to stimulate a developing genius."

There was, however, something, as it turned out: and a little later there was more. A. G. Bailey has drawn attention to the way in which Mrs. Traill became a mentor of the youthful Lampman in the days spent at Rice Lake. And the effect of *Orion and Other Poems* on Lampman's poetic development has become a familiar story. It is so germane to the central thesis of this sketch that a repetition must be risked here.

Lampman first met Roberts in the flesh as editor of *The Week*, in 1883. But he was already deeply indebted to him. Two and a half years earlier, Lampman had come upon *Orion and Other Poems*, while he was still an undergraduate at Trinity University. From that day forward, notes Duncan Campbell Scott, Lampman's life was occupied with poetry. Ten years later, in an essay never published, Lampman recalled that influence, in one of the most moving tributes ever offered to a Canadian poet: -

I was very young, an undergraduate at College. One May evening somebody lent me *Orion and Other Poems*, then recently published. Like most of the young fellows about me, I had been under the depressing conviction that we were situated helplessly on the outskirts of civilization, where no art and no literature could be, and that it was useless to expect that anything great could be done by any of our companions, still more useless to expect that we could do it ourselves.   I sat up most of the night reading and re-reading *Orion* in a state of the wildest excitement and when I went to bed I could not sleep. It seemed to me a wonderful thing that such work could be done by a Canadian, by a young man, one of ourselves.   It was like a voice from some new paradise of art, calling to us to be up and doing.   A little after sunrise I got up and went out into the college grounds.   The air, I remember, was full of the odour and cool sunshine of the spring morning.   The dew was thick upon the grass, all the birds of our Maytime seemed to be singing in the oaks, and there were even a few adder tongues and trilliums still blooming on the slope of the little ravine.   But everything was transfigured for me beyond description, bathed in an old world radiance of beauty; the magic of the lines were sounding in my ears, those divine verses, as they seemed to me, with their Tennyson-like richness and strange earth-loving Greekish flavour.   I have never forgotten that morning, and its influence has always remained with me.[1]

This stimulus was further strengthened by personal contact. When Charles Roberts came to Toronto to edit *The Week*, he and Mrs. Roberts went to live for a time with Joseph Edmund Collins, an editor and journalist who had married Roberts's second cousin, Gertrude Murphy.   Collins introduced Roberts to Lampman shortly after Roberts's arrival in Toronto, and according to E. M. Pomeroy, they at once became great friends.   The young editor of *The Week* was able to accept two of Lampman's poems, who thus appeared for the first time in a public magazine.

Duncan Campbell Scott could testify to the cultural influence of the home.   His father was a journalist and a Methodist minister, and is described as being well read beyond the round of his profession.   "In his library," the

[1]Lampman, A.: *Lyrics of Earth*.   Toronto, 1925.   Pp. 8-9.

poet son later testified, "were the standard works, translations from the classics, essays, poetry, Carlyle, Emerson, etc." His mother had a strong feeling for music, and Duncan began the study of the piano at the age of seven. He and his sisters were "happy children brought up by indulgent parents whose influence was ever for the best in letters, music and art, and who encouraged every evidence of talent."[1]

Prepared, spiritually conditioned, no doubt, by the home influence, Scott recalled that the "first perception or what might be called pang of poetry came to him in the classroom at Smith's Falls, when the master wrote on the blackboard a splash of verbal colour from Tennyson's 'Dream of Fair Women.'"

On the frontier and in the Canadian scene generally in the nineteenth century, the most favourable nest or seedbed for the nourishing of latent powers of a literary or scholarly kind was clearly the family home of the professional man. There, it would seem, social and cultural values most often combined to awake the ambition to write and publish. In such homes, at any rate, there would always be books, and a tradition of respect for education, spiritual and sometimes artistic values as well.

Wherever, in the Ontario of 1867-1900, a scholar or literary man or woman emerged, some such family setting is almost always to be found.

The biography of "Ralph Connor" is instructive. The Rev. Charles W. Gordon spent his early most impressionable years in the backwoods of Glengarry, twenty-five miles from the nearest railroad. He attended a primitive log school where learning was by rote, and little was done to stir the imagination. But other forces were more favourable for later authorship. His father, of course, had gone to university in

[1] *The Selected Poems of Duncan Campbell Scott*, edited by E. K. Brown. Toronto, 1951. P. xii.

preparation for the Presbyterian ministry. His mother, b
far the most powerful influence in his life, came of a talente
and scholarly family, being related to Robertson Smith
editor of the *Encyclopedia Britannica*, while three of her brothe
distinguished themselves in the legal profession and the publi
affairs of Quebec, and a sister became a novelist. Th
influence of the teacher in Ralph Connor's teens also appear
in his account of what he owed to William Dale, a native c
Yorkshire and brilliant Canadian student, whom by goo
chance Gordon had as his high school instructor in classic
at Zorra in western Ontario.[1]

The Osler family is another illustration, showing how
strong family clan will soften and abbreviate the cultura
shock, and permit scholars and authors to emerge even withi
a larger environment indifferent if not hostile to such develop
ment. Sir William Osler—to name the most distinguishe
member of the family—came out of an Upper Canada societ
not notable then for its intellectual or literary flavour. Bu
he was the son of a graduate of Cambridge, a clergyman
and he had access to books from the beginning. In one of hi
essays, "The Collecting of a Library," he recalled th
importance of books in his life. It is true that his father'
library of about 1,500 volumes ran heavily to theologica
commentaries, but there was livelier stuff, including books c
travel. At Weston and Toronto he had access to libraries c
scientific and general knowledge. When he was twenty h
roomed in Toronto with a Dr. James Bovell who had "catholi
and extravagant tastes" and had filled his rooms "with
choice and varied selection of books." "Three years c
association with Dr. Bovell were most helpful. Books and th
Man! The best the human mind has afforded was on hi

[1]Gordon, Charles W.: *Postscript to Adventure*. New York, 1938
Chapters II and III.

shelves, and in him all that one could desire in a teacher, a clear head and a loving heart."[1]

The sons and daughters of manse, parsonage and rectory in Canadian letters include Charles G. D. and Theodore Roberts, Wilfred Campbell, Archibald Lampman, Duncan Campbell Scott, E. J. Pratt, Ethelwyn Wetherald, Helena Coleman, Wilson MacDonald, Alan Sullivan, Robert Norwood, Ralph Connor, George A. Mackenzie, J. E. Middleton, and Sir William Osler. John Richardson's father was a surgeon, later a judge. Thomas C. Haliburton's father was a lawyer, who became a Chief Justice. Isabella Valancy Crawford's father was a doctor, as was Hugh MacLennan's. Frederick George Scott's father was a professor of anatomy, Bliss Carman's father a barrister. Marjorie Pickthall's father was an engineer.

Once the aspiring writer had left home, the stimulation of colleges, teachers, libraries, magazines and other periodical publications, literary friendships, clubs and societies, became important. There is not much evidence in the Ontario of 1867-1900 of literary coffee shops, artistic circles congregating in book-shops, or other literary societies. But at least one such association of writers is established in the records. It began when Charles Roberts accepted the editorship of *The Week*, and it later linked Roberts, Lampman, Scott and Campbell, the three Ontario poets being in some respects the outstanding literary trio of the period.

The role Roberts played as a sort of artistic father of Lampman has been related. In the same sense he could be said to be a sort of literary grandfather of Duncan Campbell Scott. When Lampman (in 1883) accepted a post at Ottawa in the public service, he soon formed a close friendship with Duncan Campbell Scott. Until the time of this meeting, Scott's interests had focussed upon music, and it seemed likely

[1]*Selected Writings of Sir William Osler.* Toronto, 1951. Chapter 16.

up to then that Scott would continue to find adequate artistic expression through that medium. The friendship with Lampman turned Scott's attention to poetry, and in due course he grew into a poet who in some respects outsoared either Roberts or Lampman. And if one wishes to trace literary great-grandchildren, it would be possible to claim John Masefield among Roberts's offspring, since it is a well-documented fact that Masefield's first poetic quickening came as a result of reading *The Piper of Arll*, by Duncan Campbell Scott. This first appeared in the New York magazine *Truth*, having been accepted through the percipience of another Canadian writer, Peter McArthur, then (1895) editor of that periodical.

Roberts resigned as editor of *The Week* after only four months, because his political ideas clashed with those of Goldwin Smith. The former Oxford don was an annexationist, Roberts a staunch Canadian Nationalist when not an ardent Tory. But in those four months Roberts played some part in the literary encouragement of other Canadian writers. He accepted and printed poetry by Bliss Carman, Elizabeth Roberts MacDonald, Pauline Johnson and Seranus (Mrs. J. W. F. Harrison). Had fate taken a slightly different turn, he might have been able also to help Isabella Valancy Crawford, who deserved and needed encouragement if any Canadian poet ever did. Elsie Pomeroy says that Roberts was on his way out to lunch on a day when Miss Crawford called with some of her poems. Unfortunately the name Crawford meant nothing to him yet, and as she was not disposed to offer *The Week* any of her work at the extremely modest rate then offered (Bliss Carman was paid two dollars for "Ma Belle Canadienne!") the casual contact never flowered into anything more. In any event Roberts left *The Week* soon afterwards, and in the autumn returned to Fredericton.[1]

[1]Pomeroy, *op. cit.* P. 50.

Beginning eight years later there was a fruitful association in Ottawa of Lampman, Duncan Campbell Scott and W. W. Campbell, as joint contributors to a literary column in *The Toronto Globe*, under the heading: "At the Mermaid Inn." Ottawa was the centre, also, of a wider literary blossoming in the 1890's, its writers finding a social outlet in an informal club which included these three and other widely-known figures of the time: W. D. LeSueur, J. H. Brown, James Macoun, Rev. Albert Walkley and A. C. Campbell.

Many writers have testified to the vital need of a receptive audience, even if very small, in stimulating creation. Duncan Campbell Scott in a reference to Lampman's earlier creative work remarks that Charles G. D. Roberts, E. W. Thomson and a few others provided the Ottawa nature poet with an "intimate circle that is essential for creative effort." Even with such a circle, and the clubs mentioned above, Lampman felt that the Canadian writer of his day was essentially alone. "The Canadian litterateur must depend solely upon himself and nature," he wrote. "He is almost without the exhilaration of lively and frequent literary intercourse—that force and variety of stimulus which counts for so much in the fructification of ideas. The human mind is like a plant, it blossoms in order to be fertilized, and to bear seed must come into actual contact with the mental dispersions of others." Frederick Philip Grove later said much the same thing: "It is a strange but indisputable thing that a work of art presupposes at least two, the one who speaks and the one who listens; the one who creates and the one who re-creates. Art is essentially the play of one soul upon another; and the ultimate material of all arts is neither clay nor colour nor form nor sound, but the recreative, responsive soul of mankind."[1]

[1] *It Needs To Be Said.* Toronto, 1929. P. 38.

CHAPTER X

THE LAST GREAT FRONTIER

FOR TWO HUNDRED YEARS the fringe of new settlement moved west across the continent on both sides of the international boundary. From the middle of the nineteenth century, an eastward advance had begun also from the Pacific. The great open plains of western Canada were the last major area of the continent to be invaded. By 1895, the American stream of settlement had occupied most of Montana and the Dakotas, and there was no more free land under the Stars and Stripes. Meantime, after the arrival of the Canadian Pacific Railway, the Canadian prairies were also filling up, slowly until near the end of the century, then much more rapidly. Vast as the plains of western Canada were, they were occupied with great speed. By 1929, most of the attractive farm lands of Manitoba, Saskatchewan and Alberta had been taken up for settlement. Frontier days in "The Last Great West" were about over.

Most of the stories of frontier settlement in the earlier part of this book have a sense of historic remoteness about them. But the frontier in the Canadian west is still a matter of living memory. The Old Timers of the earliest ranching and farming days have passed or are passing, but the children who went with their parents to the homestead country of Saskatchewan and Alberta can still recall those days with the vividness of yesterday. It is so with the writer of this book. The district between the Little Bow River and Mosquito Creek where I first lived on a prairie farm was only six years removed from the open range when I first saw it, and down in the Manyberries County a few miles from Lake Pakowki my father as homesteader ploughed virgin sod, the first man ever to farm that particular little segment of the third prairie steppe. As children in a pioneer society, we saw it all develop at first hand.

As a frontier the Canadian prairie region went through the same stages of cultural experience as other North American frontiers. Many basic similarities can be traced. But all environments are unique and all cultural invasions are different. There were elements in the frontier settlement of the Canadian West quite dissimilar to the experiences in the Maritimes, in New England or Virginia, along the St. Lawrence, or in the "Queen's Bush" of western Ontario.

So far as the early emergence of regional letters is concerned, neither the environment nor the migrating stock could, on the whole, be considered particularly promising.

Much of the range land of Alberta and Saskatchewan, to begin with, especially that part within "Palliser's Triangle," is similar in general character to the steppes of eastern Russia and western Siberia, and destined forever to be sparsely settled either by ranchers or large-scale wheat farmers. Such areas have not elsewhere in the world ever been the home of vigorous cultural manifestations of a literary type, and there was no reason to suppose that the rule would be broken here.

Though outstanding exceptions can be listed, the pioneer stocks occupying the agricultural frontier were not noted for their literary bent. Indeed, quite large and important groups among them can be regarded as definitely non-literary or anti-literary. This is not, of course, to pass judgment on their merit as settlers.

For one thing, a considerable part of southern Alberta and southern Saskatchewan was occupied by North American stock of several generations. These folk, in James Truslow Adams's figure of speech, quoted earlier, had been passed through the screen of selective settlement for generation after generation. In the process, a fine hardy breed of frontiersmen had been developed, well adapted to the grim task of occupying pioneer territory. Each generation, however, involved one more remove from the European culture from which their immigrant forebears had sprung. Among such "professional" pioneers were the Mormons from Utah, and the dirt farmers of the Middle West, from Missouri, Iowa and the Dakotas.

Again, the stream was very largely European (non-British) in racial origins. This of itself did not necessarily mean that they were less literary than British immigrants direct from the Old Country. But it *might* mean so, as in the case of the Doukhobors, the Mennonites, and the German Catholics. Even when Europeans came from an environment on a par with that of similar British immigrants, they could not escape a more severe cultural shock in transplanting. They would be likely—because of the language barrier—to require one or two generations in the Prairie Provinces, even to catch up with the British or Eastern Canadian immigrants.

If the thesis put forward in earlier pages is valid, that the emergence of native letters in any new area must await the growth and development of adequate educational facilities, publications, printers and publishers, stimulating associations of artists, and a substantial public of readers, listeners and critics, then the probability of an early flowering of prairie writers can be calculated at short notice. The chances were slim. Such prerequisites were slow in developing: some of them still do not exist today or exist in meagre measure.

The active hostility of the frontier toward such "frills" as polite letters, mentioned by Mrs. Moodie, can be substantiated by the observations of early travellers in the Middle West. Frederick Philip Grove, in his autobiography, relates that among the harvest hands in Kansas he was always careful to hide the fact that he was an educated person, that he and a partner infuriated other farm hands by discussing French poetry, and that though he always carried a few books in his pack, he "dared not take them out" at night to read. "Newspapers or even cheap magazines might have passed; but books!"

In an account of early days in Alberta, Helen McCorquodale, journalist of High River, threw light on the attitude of some of the early pioneers towards books and reading:

One pioneer woman who came west from Old Ontario in the early eighties said, "After all, our movement west was just another stage of family pioneering. My father and his brothers built their homes in Ontario out of the bush. They had come as children from Ireland, and books were not considered as necessities by those who brought their household goods across by sailing vessels. We did not have the reading habit, and our schooling was very limited. Neither books nor newspapers were a part of our lives. We didn't miss them in the west, because we had seen little of them in the east. In fact, the family Bible, with its record of births, marriages and deaths, was about the only book which many a home boasted, either in the east or in the west."

It is often told that a surprising number of our early settlers were quite illiterate when they came to this country, and this is said in no critical spirit. Education was by no means universal in the modern sense, and many of the young adventurers had been on their own from a very early age. As they became men of substance and affairs, it was part of their self-imposed labours to master reading, writing and "figgering." They learned the rudiments by secret, painstaking effort.

Senator Dan Riley recalls an amusing incident in this

connection. When he came west in 1882, after youthful
experience as a school teacher in his native P.E.I., Regina was
the end of steel. On the train from Winnipeg to Regina, he
and a fellow passenger, Bob Finnell, had agreed to be partners.
"In those days," says the Senator, "any man venturing into
the unknown west always picked himself a partner. He
mightn't have another thing on earth but he always had a
partner, so he could say, Meet my Partner! It gave him
backing in a pinch. Anyway, when we got off the train at
Regina, we began getting our gear together to head further
west by Red River cart. I had produced a box of books that
I had brought along from P.E.I.

"Bob looked at it, and was mighty disgusted when he found
it was books. He refused to have any part in such goings on.
So I left my books with a man at Regina, with instructions to
send them on to Calgary when the road pushed through. I
never did tie up with those books again. It was just as well.
They were mostly poetry, the life of Gladstone and such.
But I had turned my back on that sort of life. I was setting
out to be a rancher, and I wasn't long finding out that a man
could get a pretty bad name if he was caught reading poetry.
In fact, it was just as well not to let it leak out that he could
read and write."[1]

Homestead days in the Canadian west possessed their own
peculiar appeal and stimulus, as did the life of the wheat
villages which sprang up all over western Canada when the
railways pushed through, but there was little in them to foster
the budding literary artist. The frontier bred strong cultural
values, but they were of non-literary kinds. Edmund W.
Sinnott gets to the heart of the matter in his observation that:
"If the youngster is put into an environment where a particular
activity or value is emphasized, where others are keenly
interested in it, and where the paraphernalia for it are at
hand, it will of necessity occupy an important place in his
attention."[2] The converse is probably just as true, that if a

[1]From *The Lethbridge Herald*, December 11, 1947.
[2]*The Biology of the Spirit.* New York, 1955. P. 97.

youngster is put into an environment where *no* emphasis is given to a particular activity, where *no one* is interested in it, where *no* paraphernalia for it exists, it will occupy little or no place in his attention. The activities and values emphasized on the farms and ranches I knew as a boy, and in the villages where I worked, had little or no connection with *belles lettres*. People had other things on their minds. With rare exceptions, no one cared much for poetry, drama or essays. There was no literary paraphernalia at hand, if by that phrase Sinnott meant such things as libraries, printing presses, publishing houses and bookshops.

It is hardly necessary to recall the precise details of the general absence of such literary interests and such apparatus. The homesteaders and prairie villagers were not, of course, illiterates. Most homes had a few books, a Bible, a medical compendium, *The Sky Pilot* perhaps, a novel by Sir Walter Scott, a Sunday School prize or two. Most homesteaders subscribed to some sort of newspaper or rural magazine. The rural school library was commonly stocked with several score of miscellaneous volumes, amongst which might be a handful of English classics and an occasional title by L. M. Montgomery, Nellie McClung, Robert J. C. Stead, Charles G. D. Roberts, or Ralph Connor. The school Readers—and what fine anthologies our Readers were!—gave every child at least a casual acquaintance with some of the great English lyrics and generous selections from the prose classics.

But that summary just about exhausts the literary treasures and stimulants of the early days in the West. It was a rare and lucky child who came under a teacher who loved literature and taught it effectively. In such a favoured environment, the boy or girl might even be inspired to experiment with a few jingles or compose an ambitious school essay on the northern lights, the Chinook, or the September sunset. With such a teacher, the first feeble flights might be encouraged.

But how or where could the talent find further stimulation or any kind of public response?   The district newspaper might conceivably print an occasional juvenile effusion.   Farm magazines printed far away were the only other periodicals such children ever saw, for the most part.   Unlikely midwives, perhaps, for literary creations, which might be wedged in between cures for colic and a tirade on tariffs, but two or three rural magazines did print the verses and stories of farm children; and more than one professional writer of prairie origin will confess that it was the appearance of his or her efforts in *The Grain Growers' Guide*, *The Farmer's Advocate* or the *Family Herald and Weekly Star* that fed his ambition to do more and go further.

You could spend half a lifetime in that rangeland setting without ever seeing a play, hearing a lyric well read, meeting an author, browsing in a book-store, seeing a publisher, attending a literary society, or talking with a literary critic. In a soil so barren of literary stimuli, should vigorous growth be looked for?   What a contrast, and how remote, from the Boston of, say, 1830!

The first literature about western Canada was, as elsewhere, the work of casual visitors—discoverers, explorers, engineers, scientists, missionaries, and tourists.   It was in no sense a native literature: it was the work of men and women educated and instructed in older cultures, finding a theme in course of their travels.   There is something almost comically incongruous in the thought of James Carnegie, Earl of Southesk, composing essays on Hamlet and "remarks" on other Shakespearian plays, or analyzing one of the works of Bulwer Lytton, "while wind shook the canvas and snow sifted through the flap" of his icy tent as he camped on the prairies or in the foothills in the winter of 1859-1860.   His *Diary and Narrative* is a tale of adventure and buffalo hunting, a decade before Manitoba was carved out of Rupert's Land.   *Cheadle's*

Journal of a trip across Canada in 1862-1863, written by a graduate of Cambridge, gives some of the most vivid glimpses of the land between Fort Garry and the Rockies ever set down. Palliser's Report, Butler's *The Great Lone Land*, the familiar works of John McDougall, G. M. Grant, Sandford Fleming, and John Macoun are only the more outstanding accounts of the region between 1850 and 1880. None of these authors was a native; nor were these books in general cultural products of the Canadian West. The closest approach to native letters in those days would be the books of a missionary like McDougall, born at Owen Sound, at eighteen a teacher of the Indians at Norway House, and then for half a century a missionary among the Indians and the early white settlers.

Frontier letters in western Canada followed the familiar pattern of earlier North American experience, passing through the earlier stages more rapidly, because of the improvements in communication, but coming to a halt long before reaching a mature cultural flowering such as that of New England. No more than Montana or the Dakotas have the Prairie Provinces of Canada fostered centres of literary intensity, in which a true native literature could be easily forged. Yet, as Canada knit into a more homogeneous nation and as the barriers of distance were overcome by the engineer, talented writers of the prairies did find in Toronto, London and New York the publishers, printers, booksellers and critics they needed if their works were to find a public. A large native public was another matter. The Canadian West was slow in warming up to its own authors, even when they found favour in distant lands. The desire to buy or borrow books was limited, and the margin for such luxuries was small.

After the inevitable tales of the early travellers came the first fiction and verse, written by *émigrés* from older cultures. The sequence can be traced in Edward McCourt's account of western fiction, the most ambitious study of the subject to

date.[1] Alexander Begg, a native of Quebec City, arrived in
the West in his twenty-seventh year and spent most of the next
three decades there. His writings largely consisted of
chronicle and history, but his one attempt at fiction, *Dot It
Down* (1871), has a dubious claim to be the prairie's first novel.
Joseph Edmund Collins was a native of Newfoundland and a
friend of Charles G. D. Roberts, who used the west as a setting
for one of his novels.   The fact has some antiquarian interest,
but *Annette the Métis Spy* is prairie literature only in the sense
that Henty's *With Clive in India* is Indian literature. With
Ralph Connor we move a stage nearer.   At least he lived for
ten years in the west before he began turning out the novels of
"muscular Christianity" that were to prove so popular.
Three years after the publication of *Black Rock* (1897) the
Rev. Charles W. Gordon had become the most popular
novelist in Canada. *The Sky Pilot* found a large readership
everywhere. The author reported in 1938 that by the time
The Man from Glengarry had reached the public, the total issue
of his novels had surpassed five million copies.   This particular
literary fruition was a Canadian enterprise all the way, since
Connor's early sketches appeared in a church magazine in
Toronto, and his first book was published there.   Then came
Nellie McClung, also nurtured by Toronto editors and
publishers, with two extremely popular novels, *Sowing Seeds
in Danny* and *The Second Chance*.   Nellie McClung was not born
in the West, but she had come to Manitoba with her parents
as a girl of seven from Grey County.   Far more than Begg or
Gordon, she was a cultural product of the prairies.   Still closer
to the true native was Robert J. C. Stead, whose parents had
migrated from Lanark County in Ontario when he was but
two years old and had settled in southern Manitoba.   The
publication of such novels as *The Homesteaders*, *Neighbours* and
Grain gave the farm people of the wheat lands their first

[1]McCourt, Edward W.: *The Canadian West in Fiction*.   Toronto, 1947.

authentic portraits of people and setting by one of themselves. Compared with these, the more urbane and sophisticated prairie novels of Arthur Stringer stood out as superficial if sometimes very neat and witty impressions of the west by a literary visitor. The first unchallengable *native* novelist of the land between the Great Lakes and the Rockies was Laura Goodman Salverson, who published *The Viking Heart* in 1923. She had been born in Winnipeg in 1890. The first of Frederick Philip Grove's western novels, *Settlers of the Marsh*, came out two years later, followed by *Our Daily Bread*, *The Yoke of Life*, and *Fruits of the Earth*. There is warrant for considering Grove the most important prairie novelist, but he can hardly be claimed as a native writer, since he was twenty-one before he ever saw Canada and forty before he settled down in Manitoba. Frederick Niven, who earns a whole chapter to himself in McCourt's survey, did not leave Fleet Street until he was forty-two. Both of these men came with their cultural development essentially complete before they began their fictional studies of western Canada.

That the Prairie Provinces, despite all the literary handicaps that were listed, were to prove a more congenial soil for the nurturing of writers than was Ontario in its first century of settlement is suggested by the more recent appearance of a cluster of native authors. Sinclair Ross, born 1908, and William O. Mitchell, born 1914, were the pioneers, along with Mrs. Salverson, of those born and bred in the Canadian West. Alberta is the youngest of the Provinces in terms of settlement, and I find it interesting that of the 105 writers represented in the Alberta Golden Jubilee Anthology, no less than thirty-eight were natives of the Prairie Provinces, and several others had come to the west as infants. This would suggest that the period of the domination of native letters by the *émigré* in that region is about over.

The kinds of works produced in the earlier period also

showed a familiar progression.   The descriptive works of the
early travellers, and utilitarian productions like Palliser's
Report or John Macoun's *Manitoba and the Great North West* were
followed by sentimental and melodramatic fiction and popular
verse.   The market for subtle or sophisticated works on the
agricultural frontier was virtually non-existent.   The romantic, the heroic, and the sentimental, were strongly favoured
over the realistic or the profound.   It was idle to look for
psychological studies, novels of society and manners, delicately-
chiselled lyrics, playable drama, or literary essays.[1]   It was
idle, also, to expect much experiment or innovation.   Even
if produced, it would have met no response.   Because of the
isolation of native writers and the children of the pioneering
districts from the main forces of literary activity in other parts
of the world, a tendency to be imitative and derivative was
inescapable.   The struggling craftsmen imitated the best
models within their reach.   You can see the influence of Ian
MacLaren, Rudyard Kipling, Robert W. Service and Jack
London on a number of prairie writers.   McCourt remarks
on the tendency of early literary societies to celebrate Burns
and Tennyson and of the early versifiers to copy Browning
and Kipling.   The isolated writer is almost doomed to be a
generation or so behind the times, mastering, it may be, a
literary fashion just about the time it has run its course and
become passé and unmarketable in the livelier centres of
sophisticated culture.

Isolation from creative centres has a similar effect on all
artists, literary or graphic.   In an account of his early
life printed in a Canadian magazine several years ago, the
eminent painter, A. Y. Jackson, brought out this disadvantage
more vividly than I have seen it in any literary autobiography.
Jackson said that a visit to the Louvre in 1905 opened his eyes

[1]Lorne Pierce in The Royal Society of Canada's *Fifty Years Retrospect*.
1932.   P. 59.

to what the Impressionists had been doing, so different from "the idyllic little scenes of cows grazing and stags at bay that were considered high fashion in Montreal."

Another closely related drawback of the frontier, the distance from good teachers and good models, comes out by inference in A. Y. Jackson's reminiscences. In 1906 he went to Chicago, where "the teachers were top-rate" and "there was always the magnificent Chicago Art Gallery to browse around in. It was the first time I had been able to study the French Impressionists at leisure—the school led by Monet and Pissarro. They influenced me deeply, and for the first time I saw what could be done with landscape; I got a glimpse of how the story of the land could be told with a deep individual feeling, with all the drama of an adventure story." (Emily Carr, in *Growing Pains*, told a similar story of the transformation of her vision and technique after a visit to Paris, and at a later date to eastern Canada, when she saw what was being done by the Group of Seven.) A. Y. Jackson went on to say that while he was being inspired by the French Impressionists, Montreal was full of Dutch art, and Canadian painters were being praised for trying to paint like Corot and Constable. In a final statement which applies in part to the literary artist also, A. Y. Jackson said: "Living where we can only afford to have minor examples of the work of artists who have dominated the world, with our own artistic communities far apart, and with patrons not lavish in support of what they do not understand, we work under a great disadvantage compared with the artists in the great centres."[1] The portability and mass production of literary classics mends this situation somewhat for the writer, but the other disadvantages apply to him as much as to the painter.

The deadly effects of indifference and neglect on the one hand, the vital stimulus of a chance encounter on the other—

[1]*Mayfair*, September issue, 1954.

these can be illustrated at length from prairie literature. The literary story of Frederick Philip Grove might be regarded as a suite of variations on this theme. Grove struggled on alone in the American midwest for nearly thirty years without even finding out that publishers seldom bothered looking at manuscripts written by hand on both sides of the paper. He laboriously hammered out a working style in a language not his native tongue, without encouragement, without criticism, and perhaps without even the most useful prose models, and he paid a price for that, too. A chance encounter in a prairie village with a man who had published books put him right about the preparation of manuscripts, and the significant acceptance of *Over Prairie Trails* followed within three months. The chance presence of Lorne Pierce in a Winnipeg audience to which he read a portion of *Settlers of the Marsh* launched him as fiction author. The chance reading of *A Search for America* by the national secretary of the Association of Canadian Clubs paved the way for transcontinental tours and an editorial chair.

Before he died, Grove had met with almost endless discouragement, neglect and even open hostility, yet he persisted, produced, appeared, even if often in small editions virtually ignored by critic and reader alike. The case of Sinclair Ross is more enigmatic. "Ross has written for years with a dogged perseverance and an artistic sensitivity which deserve far more recognition than they have so far been accorded," Edward McCourt wrote in 1949, adding, sadly, "in Sinclair Ross, we may, through indifference and neglect, have permitted a fine artist to perish."

Sinclair Ross is that familiar figure in Canadian letters, a "one book" author. *As For Me and My House*, published in New York in 1941, sold a few hundred copies all told, probably a mere handful in the Canadian West. When Ross came to Ottawa shortly afterwards, a second manuscript was in his publishers' hands, but it has never appeared. It is not clear to what extent his subsequent silence was attributable to the poor reception given by the public to his first work.

The recurrence of writers who, after giving indubitable signs of outstanding promise, publish one or two books and then are never heard of again, may be a sign manual of grave literary malnutrition in any society. What is often lost sight of is that the author seldom gets into his stride with a first book, or even a second, whether he is of the highest rank of talent or not. Imagine, if Shakespeare had given up after *Two Gentlemen of Verona* or Hardy after *Desperate Remedies* or Meredith after *The Shaving of Shagpat* or Robert Browning after *Pauline*? There is a suggestive sentence or two in Somerset Maugham's *The Summing Up*; Maugham is also wondering about the young writers of promise who "so frequently fizzle out." To enrich the literature of a country, Maugham insists, you want writers who can produce a great body of work. "Of course it will be uneven, because so many fortunate circumstances must go together to produce a masterpiece; but a masterpiece is more likely to come as the culminating point of a laborious career than as the lucky fluke of untaught genius." The same law seems to apply to the musical artist. Graham George, writing in the quarterly *Culture*, has reminded us that Guiseppe Verdi wrote ten bad operas and four unsatisfactory ones before he started to write good ones. There are few Canadian writers in our literary history who were able to make a professional career of their work and keep on until the "culminating point" arrived.

The other side of the shield, the creative effect of a few words of encouragement to a struggling artist, can also be substantiated. I will content myself with two illustrations drawn from prairie writers' experiences. Nellie McClung sent a short story to Toronto in 1903. For two years its fate was unknown. Then, in June, 1905, a letter arrived at

Manitou, from the William Briggs Publishing House, signed "E.S.C.," advising Mrs. McClung that the writer had found the manuscript in a forgotten file, was impressed by it, thought it had "vitality, humour and originality," felt that the characters were "real people" and that she should "go ahead with this and make it into a book."   The writer was Edward S. Caswell.

In the moment when Nellie McClung read that sentence, a book was conceived—*Sowing Seeds in Danny*, to be followed by half a dozen other volumes.   Her career as author, in short, dated from the receipt of that letter.[1]

In *Confessions of an Immigrant's Daughter*, Laura Goodman Salverson relates her own almost hopeless struggling and squirming toward literary expression in the barren wastes of Saskatchewan village life.   It seems abundantly clear that without the encouragement of a Toronto editor, J. H. Cranston, and the praise of a Regina teacher of literature, Austin Bothwell, Mrs. Salverson might have lived and died without ever attaining important literary expression.[2]

[1] McClung, Nellie L.: *The Stream Runs Fast*. Toronto, 1945. Chapter X.
[2] *Confessions of an Immigrant's Daughter*. Montreal, 1949. Chapter xliv.

CHAPTER XI

THE FRONTIER AND TODAY

IF THE PROPOSITIONS advanced in this sketch have any validity, *belles lettres* in Canada began as a transplant from the ancient literary culture of northwestern Europe, into a soil and climate which was not, on the whole, favourable for the vigorous growth of such a transplant. Indeed, by and large, the cultural environment proved to be harsh and hostile. Other more utilitarian—and also more frivolous—flowers of society have flourished famously. Even such a cursory examination of the social history of Canada as that made in earlier chapters suggests that when the frontier days were over, the "social conditions friendly to creative composition"—the language is E. K. Brown's—were usually very slow in emerging. A more exhaustive examination of the cultural values operating in contemporary Canada might well throw light on what is being accomplished in the literary field today, and even be of some help in forecasting what might reasonably be expected in the near future. All that is attempted here, however, is a quick glance at the current scene, in the light of such principles of cultural growth and change as may be available.

Archibald MacMurchy, writing in 1906, had much difficulty, I thought, in substantiating his "conclusive" declaration that "the Canadians, though so much engaged in exploring, surveying, and cultivating the wide territories of the Dominion, are not one whit behind in the gifts of imagination and fancy which adorn the communities of the English race to be found in other parts of the world," if, in that somewhat flowery language, he meant that Canadian Literature in 1906 would stand comparison with what was being created in the United Kingdom.   Indeed, the very idea would seem to most critics to be ridiculous.   If such a literary anthologist— for there is little evidence that MacMurchy was more than a devoted collector and earnest commentator—were to tackle such a theme today he would, of course, find the *corpus* of Canadian Literature far more impressive than it was in 1906. Great strides have been taken in the intervening half century. So far as our English-language writing is concerned, a MacMurchy today would be able to add such names as Pratt, Callaghan, Klein, MacLennan, Macphail, Blake, Knister, Mitchell, Graham, Pickthall, Leacock, Grove, de la Roche, and perhaps a score of others in the field of *belles lettres*; and if he extended his survey to historical and scholarly writing, he would be able to make a most impressive collection.   In the French language, similar proud names could be added.

A library of, say, five hundred volumes, containing what is most treasured in Canadian writing today would unquestionably be a matter for patriotic pride, and I would venture to guess that at least four-fifths of the collection would bear a publishing date subsequent to 1906.

How would such a library stand the test of comparison with the recent literatures of Europe?   This is an embarrassing as well as difficult question for which I would prefer to allow our professional critics to supply answers.

Concluding a study of English-Canadian literature for 1929-1954, Northrop Frye, at the end of a list of outstanding books, judiciously remarks: "As the above catalogue implies, there is much eloquent and intelligent writing going on in Canada, without anything as yet having achieved the kind of greatness that would raise a different set of standards altogether." Desmond Pacey was more blunt in his own summing up: "It is clear from the preceding survey that Canada has produced a goodly number of talented writers; but she has not yet produced a single writer of the very first rank."[1]

These statements, read in the light of a century of speculation about the future of Canadian letters, emphasize what Northrop Frye acutely calls the Messianic note evident among our cultural nationalists. We have been waiting a long time for salvation, and even yet the mood is one of hope rather than assurance.

This state of affairs raises some interesting questions. How far have we come in Canada in accumulating the cultural and spiritual soil likely to feed a really brilliant outburst of native letters? Moreover, is the social and creative atmosphere even today at all congenial for such a phenomenon? Are there signs that it is becoming more so? Or is the trend rather the other way?

Any attempt to take the literary "temperature" of Canada today must weigh diverse and sometimes contradictory fragments of evidence. Certainly as compared with the frontier days there has been impressive progress. Canada has now moved a long way toward the educational, social and cultural conditions which might be thought to be conducive to literary creation. Whether there are still lacking two or three key

[1]Frye, Northrop: "*English Canadian Literature, 1929-1954*," reprinted in *Canadian Library*, Vol. 13, No. 3. December, 1956; Pacey, Desmond: *Creative Writing in Canada*. Toronto, 1952. P. 191.

elements before the performance is likely to be impressive is another matter.

Canadians today are a highly literate people, in the sense that a very large percentage have an opportunity to acquire considerable skill in the manipulation and appreciation of literary symbols. There are ample opportunities in a chain of libraries from coast to coast for acquaintance with the best literary models. There is no longer much excuse for a person of literary bent lacking a small working library of his own. Some emphasis is being placed by colleges on North American letters, in sharp contrast with the completely barren situation half a century ago.

It would be easy to carry these comforting assertions too far. What is available for the select few is still not available for the Canadian masses, especially those in rural or isolated areas. Many Canadian children are very unlikely ever to make personal contact with a lover of literature or a stimulating teacher of literary composition. The book is still a minor factor in Canadian life. Some revealing figures were given to the Canadian Writers' Conference at Kingston in July, 1955, by R. D. Hilton Smith. Across Canada as a whole, he said, there were fifty-seven library books for every one hundred people—"and you should see some of the books!" For over eighty per cent of rural Canada, the provision is one book for every nine people![1]

Outlets for the "literary" writer are not impressive. "Little" magazines come and go, none survives very long. Big magazines for the masses have little or no room for *belles lettres*. I am tempted to say that *The Literary Garland*, over a century ago, offered a more encouraging reception for the Canadian writer than any Canadian magazine does today. The indifference of Canadians in literary matters still gives distress to those who care about it. As recently as 1939, the

[1] *Writing in Canada*. Toronto, 1956. Pp. 116-117.

editor of *The Canadian Bookman* (Vol. XXI, No. 4) was goaded
by public apathy into writing as follows:

> After almost two years of editing and publishing, we have
> learned a lot. We imagined there was an important place
> among the publications of Canada for a magazine exclusively
> devoted to Canadian arts and letters. We know now that
> there are not enough people genuinely interested in literature
> and the creative arts in Canada to support a magazine, even so
> inexpensive as *The Canadian Bookman*. We believed that a
> young nation, jealous of its status, honours and prerogatives,
> would regard its writers and artists as indispensible to its own
> existence, and champion them as the real spokesmen and
> interpreters of the Dominion. We were mistaken. . . . At
> any rate, we have put what money we had, and all the time
> we could spare, into this venture. We sent out promotion
> copies to selected lists. Out of one thousand mailed to authors
> and learned societies, we received about ten subscribers.
> Out of three thousand mailed to book clubs, possibly a dozen
> subscriptions resulted. . . . A modest batch of ten "on sale"
> copies sent to one of the leading book stores in a university
> town was prominently displayed for one month, and all were
> returned. . . . A people with the body of a giant and the
> spirit of a cretin cannot go far. A nation without pride, a
> conscious sense of its own value and power and dignity will
> remain third-class or less. And so, in our own small way, we
> thought to lend a hand. But even our own writers and artists
> were not interested or impressed, or so we were forced to
> conclude. . . .

That was in 1939, and things are a bit better now, you may
say. For one thing, there is The Canada Council!

As compared with the nineteenth century, Canada has
built up an important book publishing industry and distributing facilities. Some account of the former has been given in
an earlier chapter. There have been several editors of
outstanding creative influence. Again it is possible to read
too much into the facts and figures of annual book production.
We publish, in all languages, about 600 titles a year, of

which four million copies are printed. This sounds well. However, it is about one-sixth of the comparable total for Belgium and about one-ninth the production in the Netherlands.[1] Any year in which half a dozen respectable novels and three good books of verse appear is a vintage year in English-Canadian letters.

The Canadian publisher does not exist to print and publish Canadian letters exclusively, of course. Indeed, his output of native works is not only a relatively small part of the total, but on the whole he tends to lose money on native ventures, or to make a lower profit than on imported products. At the conference mentioned above, John M. Gray, one of Canada's leading publishers, spelled this out as frankly as possible. Canadian writers and Canadian publishers, he said, were not to any great extent interdependent. "I doubt," he said, "that any Canadian publisher derives any important part of his revenue (or any *net* profit) from Canadian general publishing." He added that those Canadian writers who derive any important part of their income from their books (text books excepted), do not earn it in Canada and are not dependent on a Canadian publisher.

All this adds up to a rude fact, which John Gray summarized as clearly as possible: "We must face the fact that our literature lacks a rational commercial basis, and must for years to come." It is a highly successful Canadian author who makes as much from his books as a senior office boy earns in the federal government service.

Not unconnected with the plight of the periodical and book publishers is the fact that the flow of American books and periodicals across the border into Canada is by far the greatest such traffic in the world. This is also likely to continue, and even increase, for only arbitrary state action could stem the flow, and that would be folly, sure to be condemned even by

[1] See *Books for All*, a UNESCO publication of 1956, by R. E. Barker.

those who feel themselves most adversely affected by the traffic.

The distribution facilities for Canadian books across Canada do not yet appear to be impressive. The number of book-shops staffed by people who love books, who know anything about native letters, and frequented by customers of similar tastes, is pitiably small. The state of Canadian "native" publishing, and the scarcity of outlets are, of course, a reflection of general public indifference. If the interest was present, the amplified services would soon appear.

The disturbing thought is almost bound to occur at some stage: what if North American man, in F. J. Turner's famous thesis, turns out permanently to be essentially non-literary, or only incidentally interested? What if the spiritual and social soil and climate which made the great European literatures possible turn out not to be available or not even in the making on this side of the Atlantic?

For if Canadian letters have failed to live up to early expectations, have American letters on the whole, allowing for differences in population, done much better? In a survey of the cultural life of the United States, written for *Life* magazine several years ago by John Knox Jessup, there is this sweeping estimate:

The artists, like the intellectuals, have also found America repeatedly disappointing. Walt Whitman (a great exception to his own statement) once complained that America had "morally and artistically originated nothing." It is true that American art, poetry, drama, music and philosophy have somehow failed to match the American achievement in politics and economics.

André Siegfried, a shrewd European economist and philosopher, offers his own commentary on the Turner frontier thesis. In the European settlement of North America, he suggests, geography has triumphed over history. In the final section of his book, *America at Mid-Century*, he comes to grips with the possibility that the centre of Western civilization may desert Europe and become implanted in the vastness of America. If it does so, it will not exactly reproduce there the flowers of classical culture. The ideal man will become, he thinks, a man of action rather than a man of thought. "The classical tradition will still survive, but the American will be a highly developed *homo faber* rather than the *homo sapiens* as conceived by Socrates." The civilization inherited from Europe will "shed on the way shreds of contemplative spirit, something of the critical spirit of the individual, as it moves toward a new conception of human dignity, which is more social."[1] If it is true that Great Literature requires Great Men as well as a Great Society—seed as well as soil and climate—then some further words of John Knox Jessup may penetrate to the heart of the matter:

A large part of our cultural energy has gone into the democratic chore of diffusion. Never has "the best that has been thought and known in the world" been so quantitatively widespread, so available to all. There are more would-be painters enrolled in American art schools than the entire population of Florence in Leonardo's day. Our universities harbour more scholars, teachers, laboratories, projects, museums, collections, ideas and diversity of opinion than any other nation's, ever. The characteristic product of all this mass culture is what W. H. Auden calls "horizontal man," a brotherly type. It would be foolish to deny that Europe's class system has been more productive of "vertical man," the lone genius who makes intellectual history.

There are other disconcerting possibilities. From time to time we hear that this or that literary vehicle is on the decline or even on the way out. Under the heading, "No Essays, Please!", Joseph Wood Crutch recently observed that "Every now and then someone regrets publicly the passing of the

[1]Siegfried, André: *America at Mid Century*. London, 1955. Pp. 354-360.

familiar essay." Earle Birney, the Canadian poet, answering a questionnaire in 1956, said he thought that Canadian poetry was "in a declining state." He explained why. "Its poets get fewer and less productive; they are cynical about their public and the public is indifferent to them. There is no tradition left of public speaking of poetry, except (too rarely) over the CBC. . . . There is only one decent poetry magazine in Canada. A number of our best poets have fled the country and a good number of others have ceased writing. Poetry is still badly taught in the schools, often by teachers themselves badly taught. . . ."[1] In this view he was supported by John Gray, at the Conference referred to above. Of Canadian poetry, Gray said that "it was cold comfort to tell you that it seems to be in as bad a plight in England and the United States. . . . Except for the very few poets in each country who may be enjoying something of a vogue, the public has turned its back completely on poetry." He cited the case of an American poet, an unknown, but one in whom his publishers believed strongly. They promoted his book actively, and in the end sold 170 copies, or one per million in the population of the United States!

Even the novel is giving grave concern. Speaking at Ottawa in the spring of 1957, Hugh MacLennan observed that the novel was "not dying," but it was in trouble. Except perhaps for Hemingway's *The Old Man and the Sea*, MacLennan thought, not one important work of fiction had appeared in the United States since 1940. He advised writers to turn to TV scripts. Lionel Trilling can be quoted as accusing American society of lacking sufficient "social texture" to support the novel at all. John W. Aldridge contends that in the 1950's such social and philosophical writers as Dr. Alfred Kinsey, C. Wright Mills, David Riesman, Suzanne K. Langer

[1]Bulletin of The Humanities Association of Canada, January, 1957. P. 7.

and others were providing the insight into contemporary culture which in earlier decades would have been provided by the novelist.[1]

Even more radical is the idea that the book itself belongs to the past and that the new mass media will inherit the role played by it for five hundred years. It is certainly true that in large parts of the Asian world the masses are moving directly from a state of illiteracy to a cultural society kept informed by the community radio and the documentary film, with community television likely to come, and little emphasis on the printed word. It is quite possible that such societies might attain a fairly sophisticated state without much use of print, moving, as it were, directly from pre-Gutenberg days to the twentieth century, and without taking the intervening steps as we did, dominated for centuries by the products of the printing press.

The book may conceivably be doomed, but evidence so far is unconvincing. It is possible to call witnesses to contradict most of the drastic prophecies or pessimistic reports listed above. It was asserted at the Kingston Conference, for instance, that "More people are reading books than ever before." Television, on the whole, seems to benefit libraries and book reading rather than the reverse. Even Earle Birney's gloomy observations about poetry in Canada must be read alongside the view of A. J. M. Smith ("The position of the poet in Canada today is much more fortunate than it was fifteen years ago") or of Fred Cogswell ("who expressed the opinion, as an editor of a poetry magazine, that more people were reading poetry in Canada today than ever before.")

Canada's failure in the past to rise to certain challenges in the literary world has frequently been attributed to a small population and a frugal or marginal scale of living. These

[1] *The Listener*, January 31, 1957. "Art and Isolation," a broadcast by A. Alvarez.

barriers, at least, seem to be on the way to oblivion. The Gordon Commission has painted a rosy picture of future economic prospects. The population trend has had less publicity. As recently as 1946, a bulletin of the Ottawa government traced a projection of the probable population growth toward the end of the century, and calculated that a continuation of the current trend would give Canada a maximum population of 14 or 15 million by 1990, after which some decline could be expected. Such a prospect would have doomed Canada forever to give up the idea of supporting certain ambitious types of cultural institutions. But so fast have events moved that Canada passed the 16 million mark in 1956 and seems more likely to contain 30 to 35 million people by 1990. The combination of a population of that order, and the increased margin for leisure and even luxury, will pave the way for cultural ventures our grandfathers never dreamed of. The material *potentials* for a great literary era in Canada are likely to be realized. Whether the spiritual and cultural values will by then be such as to realize the potentials is a matter that it will be for the next generation of Canadians to discover.

INDEX

163

OTHER TITLES OF RELATED INTEREST